SUSTAINABLE LIFESTYLE DESIGN

*How to Not Screw Earth Over
in Your Conquest to Live Rich*

by Emily Uebergang

www.theurbanecolife.com

Copyright 2015 Emily Uebergang

Published by Emily Uebergang

ISBN: **978-0994286321**

Published: 1st April 2015

TABLE OF CONTENTS

ABOUT THE AUTHOR

Emily Uebergang is an Australian writer, blogger, and lifestyle coach. Country girl at heart and city girl by trade, her life ambitions revolve around bringing peace and nature back to modern city living. It was the world of writing that called her back to a desk; her one true creative passion. Having started her blog, The Urban Ecolife, as a means to explore her undying interest in the art of sustainable living, it has now become her breath of life. She fills her down-time geeking out over Permaculture, playing outdoors and intuitive cooking (a fancy way to say she prefers to experiment in the kitchen than follow a recipe).

Email enquiries: **emily@theurbanecolife.com**

Connect with Emily on Social Media:

Blog: https://theurbanecolife.com/
Twitter: @theurbanecolife
Facebook: https://www.facebook.com/theurbanecolife
Instagram: http://instagram.com/theurbanecolife

Cover design by **Vivian Cheng**, @blendcreations

Editing by **Joshua Uebergang**, www.joshuauebergang.com

PREFACE

"I am not a classic "eco warrior" and should confess that I'm even a little tired of words such as "eco," "green" and "ethical." It's more that I dream of a world where everything is ecological, green and ethical so that we don't actually have to define them anymore."
- Livia Firth, Eco-Fashion Activist

I don't have hippies as parents nor flowers in my hair. Dreadlocks really aren't my thing. Nor do I get around wearing T-shirts declaring my political agenda. I'm not a 70's love child; an 80's kid actually, born into an average suburban existence. The lingering expectations from previous generations for a university degree and a house mortgage hovered over my head. As a fresh university graduate tramping along through the concrete jungle in her fake leather, Chinese manufactured boots, there were only dollar signs in my eyes and TGIF on my mind. Scrounging for direction and meaning, I craved social approval in whatever form it came. I was like a caffeinated Godzilla on a rampage thrilled by the chase of glitzy toys and suited boys.

Let's just say, *sustainable living was not on my mind.*

Sitting in my fluorescent-lit cubicle browsing Pinterest boards, I wasted hours daydreaming of my next tropical island getaway, streaming the latest cat videos on Youtube and gazing out the window at the bright blue sky. *Another perfect day wasted indoors.* These mind-numbing, *brain hemorrhaging* activities were distracting me from the real problem at hand. This escapism was blinding me from reality. I failed to see that there would be no tropical island for me to escape to if I didn't stop plundering the earth, contributing to global warming and ignoring my heavy carbon footprints in pursuit of the next pay check. Blind was I because this 'at-all-cost' attitude was not exclusive. **It included my own existence**.

The wake up call came when I was working as a waste auditor to pull in some extra cash. Yes, a *waste auditor*. The things we do as cash-strapped young adults. Not the most glamorous of jobs but certainly, *one of the most eye-opening*. I was tasked with the job of sifting through corporate office garbage to report on the ratio of recycled, organic and landfill waste that was being thrown out. The heartbreaking part was seeing the endless amounts of co-mingled bags on the fast track route to landfill. Recyclable paper strewn throughout. Organic waste crying out to be returned to its home via way of a compost heap. Something was amiss. Sitting there in my office cubicle the next day, I knew I was part of this problem. Why hadn't someone told me and why was this concept so foreign to me? Looking around, people had no idea that their leftover potato crisps in their foil-lined plastic packets did not belong in the recycling bin. Even through the waste auditing job I felt helpless regardless of what I was writing down and reporting back to the CEOs because who knew if they even looked at these things. Was it just another hoop they had to jump through in order to get accredited with some green-washed logo for their website?

Word clearly wasn't getting through to those who could have the greatest impact; the you and I of this world chained to those cubicles, responsible for what went into that trash basket under our desks. Change needed to be more tangible. I needed to find a way to connect with the people on the ground level. It was this simple decision to start making changes in my own life, as small as they may seem, that has led me down a path of radical transformation that the people closest to me still laugh that this is the same girl who once only had dollar signs in her eyeballs.

Fed up with feeling encased in a glass box of emotions and sitting in a state of eternal stupor, I decided to do something. With the uneasiness of my earth tramping lifestyle resting on my conscience, I started my blog **The Urban Ecolife**. It was a way for me to formulate my own lessons and experiences as I learned more about what it meant to lead a low carbon, environmentally conscious and earth regenerative lifestyle. Call me crazy or outright lunatic but *it just felt right*. That's when the support started flooding in and people started reaching out to me expressing their similar feelings. *There are others out there!*

In each day I look for new ways to heal Mother Nature in this redemptive process. To pay off some of that debt. Despite my imperfections, I am continuously learning, but I have skin in the game now. I no longer sit on the sideline watching with a disengaged glaze over my eyes.

Can I save you some unnecessary pain in your own journey?

INTRODUCTION

"There is no reason that the universe should be designed for our convenience."
- John D. Barrow, Cosmologist, Physicist & Mathematician

Perpetually chasing this elusive 'rich life' is crushing the planet beneath our feet. Reaching for the next bright and shiny thing is like an addict getting their next hit. The moment the wave has passed, the reality hits and a depressive emptiness swallows you whole. This only leads to one outcome. **The one that leaves us in a position of deficit.**

I'm not so ignorant to say that I didn't inherit a fortunate place on this planet. You don't need to tell me twice. Was I really making use of this privilege though? *Clearly not.* Rather depressing to think about, my story is not unique. Far too many find themselves plundering the world around them in a blind attempt to make something of their life. Attempting to scrape together some feeling of success, worth, richness and happiness in accumulating things like money and possessions; ignoring the plight of the earth and their community around them. They find themselves repetitively defeated; *each and every day.* This disconnect between our present reality and its impact on our future is spreading like a virus across society. One that is peeling us away from our responsibility to this planet. Telling us that we are exempt from the laws of nature. That we are *entitled* to live carelessly. Do you see yourself in this picture?

The simple truth of the matter is this.

The health of this planet is connected to our own health and well being.

The problem?

Our generation, amongst all the fortune, have also inherited
something else far more significant - a kicker carbon footprint to boot
that would send even Beckham bending. *And here we are.*
Contributing to our own downward spiral of carbon debt to this
planet. All for the sake of narrow pursuits to live as richly as humanly
possible without understanding the impact of these decisions or even
what equates to leading an **authentically** rich life. In our pursuit for
happiness in the forms of more money, bigger houses, faster cars,
expensive clothes and extravagant parties, we've lost sight of what is
happening outside of our own little bubbles. That life you *think* you
are living, where these things make you sincerely happy, is far from
your reality and not anywhere on your horizon even if you gaze with a
pair of binoculars. In fact, it drifts further away as you stomp harder
and harder with your earth destructive habits.

Why?

You're tramping down the wrong path.

This way of living is energy draining. Not only for Mother Nature but
ourselves. When you are so deflated by your current lifestyle, you
have no mental capacity to entertain thoughts outside of your own.
Unless you intentionally seek the answers or have reality leave you a
nice surprise of a flaming bag of dog poop on your doorstep, you will
remain in the wheel of mindless consumption and bending to social
norms for a very long and painful time, along with those around you.
Churning out more carbon, more misery, and more crappy stuff into
this world.

It's time to jam the wheel.

Have you ever stopped to consider that the world around you, *and this wheel*, is crumbling and self-destruction is imminent unless we change our lifestyles now? While we may not be able to change the canvas we've been given, we do have the power to change what gets painted on there. Our fingertips wield the paintbrush. Choose your colors wisely my friends.

When I first delved into the world of sustainable living, I had this lofty notion in my head that compost was going to manifest magically without me actively involved in the process. Someone else was going to throw a life vest to the drowning Polar Bears. That I was under no obligation to recycle my milk cartons if no one was looking. Oh, and I'll forever somehow have access to affordable, healthy and chemical-free food even if local organic farmers became an endangered species. Despite reading everything under the sun on the topic and writing about these things, I was still lost. In fact, so long as I kept my dirty little habits a secret, I could go on living an earth destructive lifestyle and just hug a few trees in my spare time because *that looked good from the outside*. Only when I felt like it of course. **When it was convenient for me.**

News Flash. Our expectations for convenience have warped our perceptions regarding how Mother Nature operates. It has tainted our experiences and given us a false sense of security that this is how it will always be. Our current lifestyles we cherish so greatly will cease to exist if you don't take steps to change a few things while we have the luxury to do so.

While this is certainly not a doomsday book, I will bare the truth and yes, sometimes the truth hurts. We can no longer be ignorant to the bare facts and consequences of our existence. **Ignorance is not bliss.** It's merely setting yourself up for a harsher wake up call when the faeces really hits the fan.

I'm here to tell you that yes, you can lead a happier and more fulfilling life, a rich life in fact, even as the world stands today, *but without screwing the earth over in the process.*

What I am NOT proposing is that this will look the same for everyone. You don't have to be a bicycle riding, almond milk chai latte slurping, barefoot guitar playing, weekend farmer's market loitering hippie. If you are those things, then that's fine too! I am not going to tell you what your sustainable lifestyle is going to look like on the outside. These things, as honorable as they are, are still playing into the superficial mindset of living by a code of appearances and a set of standards that we are attempting to cast aside in this journey through Sustainable Lifestyle Design. We don't want a world of conspicuous conservationists. What matters is the transformation that occurs on the inside which will then steer your actions on the outside, *regardless if someone sees you or not.* We want a world of conscious co-inhabitants who make deliberate consumptive choices. *Teach that one to your kids.*

In this book you will learn why this is an urgent call to action and it affects not only your future, but your life as it stands now. I've broken the book into five primary sections based on timeless principles that will guide your actions and the relationships you forge with the world around you. We'll be addressing how you can make the best choices given your circumstances so they naturally become part of your thought process. From here, we delve deeply into what's happening within the realms of Mother Nature and our relationship to this problem. For how can you truly care without understanding the nature of the problem? The book includes a lengthy discussion on food because most of what we do comes back to sourcing our next meal. We need to ramp up the emphasis on protecting our vitally important food system. Other key areas we explore are simple ways you can start reducing your carbon footprint at home from day one and save money in the process.

Sustainable Lifestyle Design is a template for sustainable living that I wish someone had laid out plain and simple for me when I started on my own journey. I've spent years drowning in information and attempting to filter through what are the most impacting changes. I want to help simplify the process so people like you, aren't overwhelmed *out of action.* These are things we aren't taught in school and yet are expected to somehow fumble through life picking up the pieces. Except most people won't because we aren't having enough of these conversations. But we also need actionable steps and alternative habits that will set you on the path to living a richer and more sustainable life. **That's what helps to get people moving.**

It's about creating a one second moment of awareness that makes you pick grass-fed beef over grain-fed because that 1 kg of grain fed beef has a 30 times greater carbon footprint (and a hell of a lot of antibiotics). But getting you to a point where you don't even need to think about that. *You just do it.* Having the confidence to start your own edible food garden without fear of failing. To step up when someone needs help banding together a force of guerrilla gardeners. Understanding how to feed your body intuitively with nutrient rich foods that will have you turning your nose up at the industrially processed imitations. Practical steps you can take to incorporate new eco-friendly habits into your lifestyle that will transform how you view the world and how you live.

These habits will enhance your daily life regardless of your current circumstances. You don't even need to quit your day job. This is not about selling everything you own and moving to the remote wilderness to live amongst the wolves. I take the guess work out of how you can slot these habits into your everyday life so it feels normal and natural. It only feels like effort until it becomes habit. **This is the essence of Sustainable Lifestyle Design.**

I am embarking on a journey to make THIS our new reality and I invite you to take this giant leap of superhuman strength with me. Together, we can help each other to make radical, life changing choices and bring sustainable living to our cities. Our goal is to collectively experience a life of joy without compromising the world around us. To live a full-fledged, insanely, amazing life teamed with Mother Nature by our side. THAT is a winning combination. *Captain Planet would be so proud.*

Today it starts. You too can design your own sustainable lifestyle that doesn't screw the earth over as you live a rich life.

PART 1

UNPACKING THE PUZZLE

CHAPTER 1

The Human-Induced Carbon Dilemma

"We're becoming a planet of a thousand new major cities. The economy of the 21st century is a city-building economy. It's within our power to make it a carbon zero one, too; and to be blunt, civilization depends on our success."
- Alex Steffen, American Futurist

Carbon in itself is not evil. Let's be clear on that. It is fundamental to human existence. When I refer to carbon loosely in this book moving forward, I am referring to the atmospheric gas; carbon dioxide (CO_2). What many don't understand though, is that all this talk about greenhouse emissions, climate change and global warming (which is enough to freak out a small unborn child from wanting to exit the comfort of its mother's womb), is a result of an imbalance in our ecosystem. That is, too much human induced carbon in the atmosphere.

Carbon dioxide is quite simply a chemical compound that forms a basic building block of life for both humans and the natural environment around us. You may recall learning in school it's a natural by-product of human respiration which plants use to grow; all working together as part of this intricate ecosystem. It's formed from one atom of the element carbon bonded with two atoms of the element oxygen. Hence, CO_2. Okay, *8th grade science lesson is over.*

The impact of our rapidly growing presence on this planet has caused a huge shift in the balance of natural carbon in our atmosphere. Since the industrial age of the late 1700's, the net amount of human-induced carbon dioxide in the atmosphere has been steadily rising. As more carbon gets trapped in our atmosphere as a result of this surplus, our oceans become more acidic, extremities and fluctuations in climate become more obvious, our glaciers are subject to melting and the impact on the survival of many species, both plant, animal and human, is threatened.

Not only do we need to reduce our reliance on the unsustainable fossil fuel economy that produces more carbon than it extracts, but we need to trust in Mother Nature to do her job. Our focus needs to shift towards learning more about how to tend and care for her in order for us to coexist and not inhibit her abilities to manage the natural process of carbon balance.

Nature loves balance and it has inbuilt mechanisms to deal with the process of the natural carbon cycle, whereby it both produces and absorbs carbon dioxide. Studies show that global soil carbon stocks account for approximately three times that found in the atmosphere.[1] In 2010, our natural ecosystems, such as forests, grasslands and wetlands in the West, sequestered nearly 100 million tons (90.9 million metric tons) of carbon.[2] At first glance, that seems like a staggering number except that 36.4 billion tons of carbon dioxide were added to the atmosphere. That's a clear imbalance breaking the scales. This natural process though, remains one of the most effective ways to counterbalance the overall amount of carbon dioxide in the atmosphere; *if not tampered with*. What efforts we can go to now to preserve these ecosystems is no doubt fundamental. The mere act of planting trees and encouraging native grasslands is such a startling yet simple solution but it is still just a piece of the greater puzzle.

Even within the power of nature to counterbalance our actions, the problem exists at the point we contribute carbon emissions above and beyond to which nature can handle. By continuing to live energy intensive lifestyles while planting a few trees in your spare time, you're not addressing the root problem but merely participating in reducing the symptoms. It's like bandaging a broken arm but attempting to continue playing tennis with it. The short answer;

reduce your personal carbon footprint. As David Holmgren explains in his book, Permaculture: Principles & Pathways beyond Sustainability, *"The rise of individualism in the modern world makes possible personal expression and action through lifestyle choice, even if few choose to do so in any more than superficial ways. The empowerment of the individual provides a unique opportunity for bottom-up change."*

The efforts you go to in order to mitigate the root cause will significantly help to relieve the symptoms of climate change.

CHAPTER 2

Climate Change Skeptics Are A Dying Breed

"I have a theory about global warming and why people think it's real. Go back 30, 40 years when there was much less air conditioning in the country. When you didn't have air conditioning and you left the house, it may in fact have gotten a little cooler out there, because sometimes houses become hot boxes. Especially if you're on the second or third floor of a house in the summertime and all you've got is open windows and maybe a window fan. Or you have some servant standing there fanning you with a piece of paper. When you walked outside, no big deal, it's still hot as hell. Now, 30, 40 years later, all this air conditioning, and it's a huge difference when you go outside. When you go outside now, my golly, is it hot. Oh. Global warming. It's all about the baseline you're using for comparison."
- Rush Limbaugh, American Talk Show Host

When we start using our air-conditioning systems as a baseline to argue *against* or legitimize climate change over the scientific data, that's when you know we've somehow failed each other as a society. The aforementioned quote from Rush Limbaugh, an American radio talk show host and political commentator, is, unfortunately, a very dismal reflection of public thought at large. How can we still be in denial when 97% of peer reviewed climate change studies, taken from 11,944 climate abstracts between the years 1991 – 2011, endorse the consensus that humans are causing global warming?[3] If you don't think this is your problem, then think again. *"Nobody on this planet is going to be untouched by the impacts of climate change,"* explains Rajendra Pachauri,[4] chair of the IPCC, upon the release of the UN's climate science panel's most recent 2014 Summary Report for Policy-makers.[5]

Climate change skeptics are a dying breed. **Do you still manifest**

doubts? My word of advice - *don't be the last one left on the dance floor when the Congo-line has well and truly danced on.*

You exist on this planet alongside over 7 billion other humans. How is that for a slap in the face? Yes, you are only one of 7 BILLION souls as it stands today. So can you begin to imagine the environmental pressure an additional 2.5 billion souls will have on this planet if we continue to live as we are? By 2050, those numbers will be our reality.[6] Now consider the enumerable number of other species on this planet in all their glorious forms; from plants to animals to micro-organisms. These are not numbers we can count on our hands, nor a problem of how to manage that we can turn our backs on. We aren't the only species on this planet who are scrambling for survival. The bitter truth? Their survival doesn't depend on us. **Our survival hinges on theirs**.

What would the world look like if all 7 billion of us were driving Humvees to the supermarket to buy our groceries? Even a fifth grader could tell you this is not viable and yet so many of us still do, and even feel *entitled* to do so in the process. After all, it's your hard earned cash that brought you that right. *Right?* Or what if all 7 billion of us lived in McMansions with pristine chlorine swimming pools and fertilized lawns? Another rather implausible scenario but many still place this goal on the pedestal of human accomplishment to work towards and provide them feelings of success, richness and self-worth.

Mull this over for a moment. What entitles one person to experience these luxuries while another suffers on the brink of non-existence, drowning in pollution and toxic contamination from the outsourced externalities of these grand lifestyles? Just because the pile of trash is not on your doorstep, does not mean it doesn't exist.

I'm not attempting to inflict layers of guilt upon your conscience. What we need to do is challenge our perspective on life and understand that our decisions have consequences and some come with greater negative consequences than positive. From the brand of toothpaste you buy to the decision of whether you upgrade your car to that luxury convertible.

Imagine a world where the mere act of walking down the street is turned into a severe health hazard due to toxic air pollution. *Well*, this is already happening and it's coming to a city near you. The World Health Organization (WHO) reports that just 12 percent of the world's city dwellers are breathing clean air.[7] Around half are exposed to air pollution at least two-and-a-half times what is considered 'safe' levels (which is 25 micrograms of airborne particulate matter). So you don't have to be living in India's capital, Delhi, which has pollution six times the safe limit,[8] to get your daily dose of toxic pollution. Londoners alone get their fair share breathing in more than 1.6 times the recommended safe level according to this same WHO report. Among some of the most polluted cities in the world are those that house more people than the whole population of Australia.

Traveling through China some years ago, I caught myself (on numerous occasions) gawking at the number of citizens who were sporting face masks as part of their daily attire. And they weren't trying to make a fashion statement either. It's a necessity for the sake of their lungs. Even during my short time there I was blowing black snot out of my nose. China's youngest ever lung cancer patient died in November 2013. She was only 8 years old. Air pollution was to blame. It's not uncommon in Northern China for school to be called off due to 'smog days.' The Blacksmith Institute released a report stating that industrial pollution poses a health risk for more than 200 million people around the world, often through elevated levels of cancer, respiratory disease and other illnesses.[9] How long do you expect to outrun a similar fate? If you live in a high density urban area, your lifestyle is under threat. You can eat all the kale you want, but it won't account for much if you choke on everyday air. Pollution is is not only affecting the environment. It's directly compromising your own health.

So I've scared you away from the thought of living in the city, have I? Maybe you'd prefer to escape to a remote tropical island or a hidden cabin nestled in some remote mountain ranges. *Good luck my friend.* If we continue to live as we are, the only options for your getaway or vacation may involve visiting the local mall or a museum that tells stories of ancient prairie lands, flourishing green mountains and crystal clear glacial lakes. In this 'fantasy' world, they no longer exist of course. They simply can't under the circumstances. By this point in time, we will have stripped the earth bare of it's natural resources, killed off the ecosystems it supports and contributed to exorbitant amounts of toxic pollution that causes atmospheric imbalances. Then there's the slight matter of having enough country acreage to house 7 billion people and counting. Another path that leads us to the same conclusion.

Do you want to live in a world where we no longer have any exotic islands to vacation on because the oceans swallowed them whole? Do you want to rely on manufactured gruel depicted in sci-fi movies to satisfy your insatiable appetite because we failed to care for and regenerate the earthly, nutrient rich topsoil to sustain our food crops?

For the first time in history, the next generation is facing a life expectancy of 5 years less than the previous.[10] Our longevity and health is diminishing despite medical advancements because degenerative lifestyle diseases have taken the number one spot as health killers. Our current lifestyles are killing us.

Is this the kind of world you want to live in?

This is a wake up call. We are treading along that crumbling path to such a future. All the while, you remain cooped up inside your apartment, streaming the latest episode of The Game of Thrones, oblivious to the war raging outside between man and nature.

Within my beloved home country of Australia, our natural landscapes are some of the most unique and isolated on the planet. Even with just a small rise in earth surface temperatures, they are at severe risk as we face the most extreme weather conditions on record. The Australian Bureau of Meteorology was even forced to add a new color to its weather maps to reflect these rising temperatures. We're already seeing the impact climate change has had on Australia's Great Barrier Reef, one of the seven natural wonders of this world. Since 1985, it's lost over half its coral and natural biodiversity.[11] Professor Ove Hoegh-Guldberg, who heads up the Coral Reef Ecosystems Lab at the University of Queensland, says, *"A global reduction in carbon dioxide emissions is the long-term key to preventing bleaching and reducing the intensity and volume of storm systems. What we do in the coming decade will ultimately determine the future of ecosystems like this one."*[12] **What we do now matters!**

A study conducted by the University of East Anglia found that more than one half of the plants and one third of the animals will see a dramatic decline by 2080 if nothing is done to reduce the amount of global warming and slow it down.[13]

If you aren't impressed by these figures, then consider the economic ramifications. Global warming is already costing the world more than $1.2 trillion a year, wiping 1.6% annually from global GDP.[14] This same study associated over 400,000 deaths a year to the effects of climate change. If you are of the mind that this is happening in some far off country and of no concern to you, it's time to shake yourself out of your denial coma. The cost of fuel, food and energy will continue to rise as these resources become more scarce and governing agencies exert further control in desperate attempts to keep their hands on the wheel.

The National Climate Assessment of the US released a report stating, *"Climate change, once considered an issue for a distant future, has moved firmly into the present. Summers are longer and hotter, and extended periods of unusual heat last longer than any living*

American has ever experienced. Winters are generally shorter and warmer. Rain comes in heavier downpours... Residents of some coastal cities see their streets flood more regularly during storms and high tides... Hotter and drier weather and earlier snow melt mean that wildfires in the West start earlier in the spring, last later into the fall, and burn more acreage." This story is being repeated all around the world.

The Pew Research Center published a study that revealed only 40% of Americans considered global climate change a "major threat". More troubling to Americans were North Korea's nuclear program (59% called it a major threat), Islamic extremist groups (56%) and Iran's nuclear program (54%).[15] In a society more preoccupied by offshore nuclear war programs, we are oblivious to the destruction happening in our own backyards.

Clearly our priorities need to be realigned with the reality at hand. As a co-inhabitant of earth, we need to be accountable for our choices. We need to acknowledge that our actions today will have an impact on our way of living in the years to come. If we act boldly now to cut our climate pollution, we can avoid the major threats to human security and protect vital ocean systems, forests and species. The choices we make today will define how history will judge us tomorrow.

> *"You cannot escape the responsibility of tomorrow by evading it today."*
> - Abraham Lincoln

We need a good slap on the forehead or knuckle punch in the gonads to bring us back into reality and to keep this agenda as a blinking red dot on our mental radars. Within you lies a spark that's ready to ignite. Imagine changing the course of planetary sustainability one conversation at a time. Perhaps together we can start a process we can call 'sustainable back-burning' to save our landscapes. With a little kindling to assist, we have the power together to crank up the internal thermostat so public bodies feel the heat of responsibility to make urban sustainability *de rigueur.*

If you're like me, then you genuinely enjoy the urban lifestyle. It's a melting pot of culture, with all it's liveliness, variety, convenience and opportunities; minus the vehicular fumigation of our species. This is our reality. Yet, you stand divided. You can't ignore the other side of the story; the pull of social pressures to earn a decent living, climb the corporate ladder and make something of your life worthy of applause. All the while your inner self yearns for that sense of simplicity which our ancestors experienced. Free from the stresses that come with the urban lifestyle and modern living. To live in harmony with nature, to respect the land, to be enriched by a sense of community, to wake each morning feeling that you are connected with nature and doing something virtuous with your life.

CHAPTER 3

The Suffering of Mother Nature

"This we know; the earth does not belong to man, man belongs to the earth. All things are connected like blood that unites us all. Man did not weave the web of life, he is merely a strand in it. Whatever he does to the web, he does to himself."
- Chief Seattle, Respected Duwamish Chief

When we stop to contemplate the purpose of the global suffering that surrounds us, there are not many solutions. Our current way of thinking will have us blaming, shaming and inflicting guilt on others. Do any of these things change the end result? *Of course not.* While the world may seem like a cruel place, if we shift our perspective, it can also be a beautiful and awe-inspiring place of peace and opportunity. This is not to ignore the suffering around us but to acknowledge that as we mourn and suffer, Mother Nature too cries in our wake.

"What we are doing to the forests of the world is but a mirror reflection of what we are doing to ourselves and to one another."
- Gandhi

Our own suffering is so intriguingly intertwined with that of the world's, is it no wonder that our self-abuse is reflected in the abuse of nature? By acting on these destructive tendencies, you are dragged further and further from the things in life that bring you sincere fulfillment and joy. From your family and friends, love, peace, and your connection with Mother Nature. Suddenly, you find yourself lacking room for such experiences. Your mind and heart becomes a barricaded fortress. It's a self-fulfilling prophecy and a sick cycle to be trapped within. Where we forgo self care, we in turn neglect our responsibilities to the greater world. Our identities become disconnected until little else remains than a hollow shell.

At the deepest and darkest moments in my own life, from the outside, I probably looked like I had my life completely together. I had a steady job with a decent enough income. While my health and fitness was mediocre, I had no stabbing pains or obvious health ailments, so who was I to complain? I wasn't actively involved in my community except through participating in countless social activities that keep me drunk on life and numb from feeling what was really going on inside my head. While I wasn't purposely trying to drag the world down, I certainly was indirectly influencing it in this way because of the crappy thoughts and negativity I was putting out there.

In one word, **I was complacent**.

Despite this charade of supposedly *having it all together* and feeling like I really shouldn't have anything to complain about, I couldn't shake off the shame and negativity that plagued my thoughts. Being honest with myself, I was depressed about my disconnected work life, feelings of a future with no direction, how many pounds of emotional baggage I had gained in the process, and feeling like a stranger, not only within my own body, but within my own community. I retreated into a dark cave of self loathing. The more isolated I became, the more I would stew on these feelings, manifesting them even greater. Even in the presence of loved ones, I was overwhelmed by the drowned out thoughts in my head and struggled to feel connected to what was going on around me. In these moments of life I remember how hard it was for me to think beyond my own immediate needs. This bubble was warping my experiences; blurring my vision while those around me attempted to pop it with the needles of love and support. I was so fixated on what I didn't have in life, my flaws and countless deficiencies, even if they did manage to pop my bubble for a moment, I would no sooner create a new one.

The realization came when I finally acknowledged I was waiting for someone else to do the hard work for me. Not only to provide solutions for the world's problems, **but for my own problems**. I didn't understand the power within my own hands to start creating the radical shift I so desperately craved. All I saw in the world were problems because that's what I had trained my mind to see. The more chaotic my episodes became, the harder I needed to scramble in order to control the uncontrollable in my life. In the process, I was forgoing my responsibility to the only thing I had power over to control. **Myself**.

It was the transformation *from within* that changed the direction of my life. A complete mindset shift. I was the only person who could lead that. The more I opened myself up to change and made concerted effort to shrink my circle of control (and letting go of what I couldn't), the easier it became. There were of course challenges. At times this involved *forcing* myself to just get outside and participate in life again. What it comes down to is understanding that the only person who can change the course of your own life is you. It's through this process that you give permission for those around you to make changes and it's how you can then influence a more positive world.

There is no magic pill to wipe away a life of pain. Just like we can't expect to heal Mother Nature over night, we can't expect to wake up tomorrow and have it all figured out. **It's a daily practice.** A practice that involves giving things a go, making mistakes and then giving it another go. I share my experiences with you to instill hope. Sometimes we just need to do *something* to get us out of a slump. You are not alone in these challenges and there will be days when you feel exhausted, mentally drained and as though you have no influence over the future of this planet and everything you do accounts for nothing. Rest assured that even the slightest shift in your life's trajectory can cause an earthquake of change. You just need to be comfortable with the fact that you can't control *every little detail*. Your actions, however, **significantly** influence the process and magnitude.

Sustainable Lifestyle Design teaches us to embrace change. To not resist it because what we resist persists. If our focus is solely on resistance, then all we will see from nature is resistance. It's like telling a blind man to look harder. We need to look at the world from a different angle and relinquish these feelings of control and mastery in order to be more effective in our purpose. To restore our trust in Mother Nature as we step back and embrace our role as stewards. *Not as micromanaging control freaks.*

CHAPTER 4

Man vs Wild: Who Will Reign Supreme?

"In short, a land ethic changes the role of Homosapiens from conqueror of the land-community to plain member and citizen of it. It implies respect for his fellow-members, and also respect for the community as such."
- Aldo Leopold, Author of 'A Sand County Almanac'

Whilst this current destruction of nature is far beyond that witnessed in history before, it is not completely foreign to man's character. The human species is well known for its self-destructive attitude. Mother Nature can attest to this fact. How is it that every other living thing in nature leans towards a behavior of survival above all else, while we lean towards pillaging?

History has repeated itself over and over as civilizations have set out to command and conquer, and this is even *among our own kind!* Jared Diamond's book, 'Collapse', explores how some of the "greatest" civilizations in human history faced the same inevitable fate; self-destruction. Due to a lack of respect, understanding and pro-activeness to sustain the very environment that supported them, they wiped themselves out. **Is this what we define as success and progress?** Are we steering our current civilization towards a similar fate?

It's rather ironic these much applauded 'great' civilizations of human history that accumulated the most wealth and pursued a reckless attitude of conquering the world, were considered the most powerful of their time. Yet they cease to exist . Many of the traditional cultures and native tribes who have survived the test of time are those who understand the natural limits to growth. Those who live with the land in a respectful, humble and sustaining manner.

For a large chunk of us though, especially within the Western world, we've *lost our way*. Somewhere along the way we must have dropped the little pamphlet that was being handed out during creation with the instructions of how to be good stewards of this planet.

We need to raise the white flag and surrender this attitude of destruction. *Kill the weeds, kill the pests, chop down the trees, kill this, kill that.* To build and build, to plunder and claim, and to build some more while we're at it. Take a look around at the damage we've done to this planet in the process. Man acts as though our sole purpose in life is to gain mastery over the planet. To what end does this purpose serve?

Where we plunder the earth and strip it of its ability to regenerate and sustain itself in its natural way; we have placed our own short term interests before life itself. The catch here though, is in doing so, we are inadvertently jeopardizing our own quality of life and our own futures.

Can I get all nerdy and "Avatar" on you for a second. Do you remember how the Na'vi warriors have an admirable respect for Mother Nature and its creatures? They gave thanks for everything, even in death. They understood that they were merely a small piece of the bigger picture rather than the be all and end all.

As the Na'vi were, so should *our* attitude be. The natural world can quite go on living without us as it's a self-sustaining system. We have been blessed with a life-supporting environment for ourselves to flourish and multiply within but under the conditions that we tend to it and maintain it.

Now you may say in response, *but I didn't sign up for any of this* and right you are. This is not something you sign up for. There is no sign-up sheet hanging in the lunch room petitioning for your signature. It's an innate responsibility we should accept as custodians of this land and it's in our best interests to do so.

The Greek origins of the word Ecology is *"oiko"* which means *"house"* and *"logos"* which means *"the study of"*. Ecology means '**the study of one's house**'. Caring for something requires you to have an understanding of its operating environment and it is through ecology that we have come to understand and appreciate the interconnectedness of man to nature. I do believe that this is an innate desire within each and everyone of us; to feel connected to this world and to feel a part of it. This responsibility falls in the hands of every human being who calls earth home regardless of the who or where.

You would not release a sewage pipe in your living room nor dump landfill in your backyard, yet this is what we do to our earthly home when neglecting ecology. Caring for ourselves requires understanding and caring for the planet. **This should be priority.** Everything that comes after this, the luxuries of entertainment, hobbies, Facebook, denim jeans, pogo sticks and popsicles; *we need to keep in perspective.*

CHAPTER 5

Biomimicry: Learning from the Wisest Sensei

"Look deep into nature, and then you will understand everything better."
- Albert Einstein

I first stumbled upon the ideas of Biomimicry through the writings of Janine Benyus. The underlying principle of her book, '*Biomimicry: Innovation Inspired By Nature*,' is to innovate based on nature's extensive design experience. Humans have been replicating nature's greatest designs for centuries. We've observed the way plants harness energy through the process of photosynthesis as inspiration for the creation of solar panels. Swimming flippers mimic the very features that make dolphins such effective swimmers. When you observe the natural river systems that sustain thousands of precious micro-ecosystems; man-made waterways pale in comparison but reflect this network. Even the intricate process of a beaver building a dam has provided the basis for man to recreate this process on a monstrous scale.

We can use our skills of observation and gain inspiration from these natural structures, ecosystems and patterns of design in our own lives. Nature teaches us that the solutions to our problems needn't be as complicated as we make them out to be. Bigger is not necessarily better. That we should recycle everything. Waste not a thing. To focus on biodiversity and most importantly, use only the amount of energy that is necessary.

What is being called for is to bridge the worlds of nature and technology. We already have access to all the skills and all the know-how to make changes today. You don't need to wait for some radically complicated and technologically advanced pollution vacuum to save the day.[16] Who's to say that "someday" will come and be what you expected? My mother would promise me "someday" when I begged for things. Sorry mum, *but I still don't have my pet pony.*

This problem can't wait until "someday" when technology catches up to remedy the symptoms and pick up the mess of pieces. We need to act in prevention. It may not sound as sexy as the latest techno-whiz device, but Mother Nature is the one who has withstood the test of time and who possesses the greatest accumulation of knowledge and experience for us to learn from. This needn't discount the need for human innovation. By leaning on nature's sustainable design systems, we can utilize the skills we have, of taking an idea and turning it into something practical, to get us the desired result. We are being called to address the fundamentals flaws of our existing systems and designs, and look closer to nature for answers moving forward.

CHAPTER 6

The Progress Myth: The Rotten Truth of Modern Society

"Usually, terrible things that are done with the excuse that progress requires them are not really progress at all, but just terrible things."
- Russell Baker, Newspaper Columnist & Author

What do you consider to be human progress?

The dedication of untold natural resources and taxpayers dollars to the building of grand monuments and sculptures that commemorate historical moments of social progress all the while the poor are left begging at the footsteps? Large cement, carbon producing buildings that stretch for as far as the eye can see but with few (if any) carbon extracting, food producing 'green-scapes' lining the streets? The genetic modification of natural plant species that create an earth degrading dependency on chemical fertilizers, herbicides and pesticides to maintain their so call 'radical technologies and efficiencies'? Bulldozing endangered rainforests that support delicate and abundant ecosystems in order to make way for unsustainable monoculture crop like GMO soy and corn that feeds into the sick food system we're attempting to combat?

I challenge you to question this mainstream notion of what is applauded as being "human progress."

Tearing up land in order to make way for human "progress" - *this is nonsensical.* Crushing natural biodiversity in the namesake of a few greedy individuals - *this is nonsensical.* Rationalizing the marginalization of minority groups within society to maintain a tradition of social slavery - *this is nonsensical*. Where there is progress through one's eyes, **there's regress through another's.** It just depends on which side of the coin you happen to be tied to.

Such war cries towards "progress" are so ludicrous at times that they cloud our focus from the social goals that most of us are really trying to achieve. Things like good health, freedom, education, safe community, access to clean water and sustainable food. The pollution, the environmental destruction (and the lack of accountability to such things), the addictive greed and the social divisions; these things are what causes rifts in society that only hinder us from sharing real freedoms with others.

Man has a tendency to pit himself against this elusive notion of an enemy we refer to as "them." Who is this enemy that warrants our own self-destruction? It just goes to show we don't even understand the nature of this eternal battle for human progress if it creates more problems for ourselves. This narrow-minded thinking that we have a life of our own to preserve all the while destroying everyone else's in the process; *it's delusional.*

We don't need to be at war with each other or with the world around us. The sooner we find peace with nature, the sooner we can find peace within ourselves. There is no "fight" to win. This fight is merely a figment of our imagination; something we've construed in our own minds. Nature is not out to get us, unless of course, you purposefully put yourself in harms way of a mothering bear or a shark feeding frenzy. That, my silly friend, *is your own fault.*

CHAPTER 7

The New Economy: Embrace Change or Stay the Same?

"Our modern society is engaged in polishing and decorating the cage in which man is kept imprisoned."
- Swami Nirmalananda, Master Yoga Teacher

The economy is set to change. As we tap into nature's limited oil reserves and run them dry, we need to prepare for a different future. History has proven that the most resilient cultures are those who have flexibility, adaptability and diversity built into their core. Much the same can be said for the success and resilience of businesses as their economic operating environments continue to rapidly evolve. It was drilled into me during finance class that the foundation of a good investment is to *'diversify, diversify, diversify.'* This same principle can be applied to most areas of life. From the food you eat to the plants you choose to grow in your garden, and not being reliant on one job prospect.

We see people, loved ones even, falling victim time and time again to stock market crashes, business failings, job cuts and a whole season's worth of crop being wiped out by disease or pest infestations. Disappointment because their expectations weren't reached. We've mastered the art of deluding ourselves into believing that the good times will keep rolling; that we're somehow immune to the laws of nature. When we don't have self-resilience built into our lives and we haven't diversified our risks, then we are far more susceptible to even the slightest shift in external economic pressures.

If this gravely concerns you, the fact that things won't forever be the same, you may need to turn down the bright lights in your life, remove the comfy cushions and get off that oh-so-thrilling high horse you're riding on. The more open and adaptive you are to this reality, the less frightening and difficult change will be for you.

"I think we risk becoming the best informed society that has ever died of ignorance."
- Rubén Blades, Latin Jazz Musician

"What goes up, must come down" is not only the universal law of gravity but a universal law of nature. As humans, we do not stand apart from this. The growth of a plant from seed to fruit and eventually decay, is reflected in our own lives. We reach our peak of youthfulness before degeneration sets in. The degree to which we support our health will determine how drawn out and painless (or painful) this process will be. It's only natural for global economies to fluctuate between peaks and troughs operating within this realm of existence. As witnessed during our most recent economic crisis, some countries hit rock bottom harder and faster while others found another, more sustainable, new plateau to operate within until the next cycle hits.

This story is best described by David Holmgren so I won't attempt to reinvent the wheel. He eloquently says,

"When we picture the energy climax as a spectacular but dangerous mountain peak that we (humanity) have succeeded in climbing, the idea of descent to safety is a sensible and attractive proposition. The climb involved heroic effort, great sacrifices, but also exhilaration and new views and possibilities at every step. There are several false peaks, but when we see the whole world laid out around us we know we are at the top. Some argue that there are higher peaks in the mists, but the weather is threatening.

The view from the top reconnects us with the wonder and majesty of the world and how it all fits together, but we cannot dally for too long. We must take advantage of the view to start our way down while we have favourable weather and daylight. The descent will be more hazardous than the climb and we may have to camp on a series of plateaus to rest and sit out storms. Having been on the mountain so long, we can barely remember the home in a far-off valley that we fled as it was progressively destroyed by forces we did not understand. But we know that each step brings us closer to a sheltered valley where we can make a new home. "[17]

I see three options in this scenario. You can base-jump face first off that cliff into a new existence which would certainly be the quickest option. It's also the most scariest and potentially isolating. Few follow this path but their learning curve is steep and let's just say, it's not for the faint-hearted. Think about those who sell everything they have, quit their jobs, and take off on a new journey of self-sufficiency.

The second option is the one Holmgren describes. You've experienced the high from the altitude and enjoyed the scenic view but seeing a dangerous cloud brewing in the distance, make the decision to start the journey to safety. You give yourself the time to take short stops along the way and breathe. The journey is certainly more graceful and provides ample opportunity to get yourself together. These are the people who are slowly but surely finding ways each and every day to incorporate more sustainable lifestyle habits and changes into their lives. A process that builds self-resilience.

Don't be in the third camp of people. The ones who linger too long, soaking up the ego-fed, mental applause for their achievements. Where pride, not the altitude, gets to their head and they dally for *just that little bit too long*. Then suddenly it's too late. The clouds are upon them and the weather too unpredictable. The descent is fraught with danger and for some, it may even be too late.

Our existing economic system teaches us to abide by the rules, follow the social norm, do as is expected, and the system will reward us and take care of us.

How is that working out for you?

News flash. That system is broken. It's been broken for years. At some point in time it may have worked but times have changed. There are billions who have been left behind who couldn't care less for the system. Nor could Mother Nature for that matter. The only ones who care for the system are those benefiting from the system. We're sick, fat and tired. Exhausted and overwhelmed. Confused and deranged. *And this is at the best of times.*

I found myself trapped in this same wheel as a fresh university graduate. Clearly success was written in my stars, *or so I thought.* I had followed the recipe. Get good grades, get to university, get a good job and then I would be sailing on the high seas of life. The batter had been pre-prepared for me, neatly sealed in plastic packaging with instructions affixed. All I had to do was fold it all together and pop it in the oven. The end result being a light and fluffy sponge cake. *Except someone had forgotten to include this part in the fine print.*

You see, **I hate sponge cake.**

It lacks substance. No one was teaching me how to create my own recipe. Everyone just wanted to preach at me to follow the steps. Through trial and error, I came to discover I enjoyed the process of crafting together my own dense, gooey, double-fudge chocolate mud cake more than the airy, tasteless and generic approach. Life is not a one size fits all. At least if I make my own recipe, I can have a delicious batter to lick from the bowl in the process *regardless* of the end result.

Life starts and finishes the same for everyone. Firstly you are born, and lastly you die. It's about how you fill in that time in between that really matters and there's no set recipe for that. There shouldn't be. You don't derive worth by following due diligence, signing the contracts and fulfilling the status-quo character profile.

The system supported by the current world view is one that has two sides to its coin. It's a game of winners and losers; a world of trade-offs. In this game of coin toss, there can't be a winner without a loser. And by whose rules do you think we are playing?

For far too long, the winners have dictated the rules. Rules that have merely contributed to the growing wedge between social classes which leaves the underclass forever scrapping at the bottom of the barrel. Rules that uproot the few remaining trees while the earth continues to erode around us. Rules that protect the interests of an elite few who have so much already while whole species are wiped from existence each day.

But alas, *no longer.*

The biggest problems also have the potential to provide us with the greatest solutions. Within your grasp we have the answers. Look around you. The very things that surround you on a day to day basis have a far more powerful impact on this overall picture than we give them credit for. From what food is in your fridge, to the kind of clothing you wear, the decor that adorns your living room and the television programs you watch that infiltrate your mind. The accumulation of these things define your lifestyle.

Too often we rely on chance and fate to get us through each day rather than moving each footstep with intention. The sooner you move past your own little mind games, the sooner you can move forward. Mother Nature isn't into games. She especially doesn't care for our games.

Where those who revel in the success of their yesterday, will likely fall flat on their face as the world takes back her claim. I am not making this statement as a threat. It's merely a collection of thoughts from the stories I've heard, observations of the world that I've grown up in and the voices of those crying out around me. Those who outwardly deny, refute and choose to rebuke, are making a choice to and so be it. That's their decision to make. The thing is, we don't have time to entertain their arguments and skepticism. We have better things to be doing with our time, like planting seeds, growing food and helping others to build self-resilience into their lives.

What we have time for are those who are willing to explore the possibility that there *is a better way to live*. Those people who are humble enough to say that we don't need to have all the answers in order to start doing something today. The ones who are willing to step up to the plate in pro-activeness. Those who are open to a way of living that is at peace and harmony with nature and each other. **We need more of you.**

Why wait when you have more to lose by not doing anything than what you stand to gain by taking action now?

It's a voluntary position anyone can uptake. We are at a point in time where we have a choice as to how we can approach this problem. Many of us are fortunate enough to yet be forced into a dire situation where we have no choice but to give up our luxuries because the earth is crumbling from beneath our feet.

PART 2

UNRAVELLING YOUR LIFESTYLE

CHAPTER 8

Richie Rich: The Money Myth Wringing You Dry

"If you want to feel rich, just count the things you have that money can't buy."
- Proverb

Living rich has nothing to do with the number on your bank statement. You can't place a price on time nor on your relationships and experiences. **These are things money cannot buy.**

To really extract the most out of life you need to redefine what exactly it means to live richly in accordance with your personal value code. Think back to your happiest memories in life. Who were you with? What were you doing? My heart literally explodes when I spend time in nature, whether that be swimming in the ocean of hiking mountains. Couple that with the company of those I love and you have one happy girl. From this, I can say that my personal value code in experiencing a rich life is one where nature and relationships underpin my existence.

Let's be honest with ourselves for a moment. We understand that the current economic system we live within, our primary form of trade requires money. It's our present socially accepted currency. This may change in time but for now, it's what we have to work with. In order to earn money, we are required to work. While there are certainly less conventional ways that allow us to do this, for most of us, this involves working in jobs that suck more than the life out of us, but the life out of your health, free time and relationships. Whether that be a relationship with loved ones or Mother Nature. It may even be a job that doesn't jive with your personal value code. While I'm not about to scream at you to quit, *although I'd highly suggest you start looking for ways to reshuffle your priorities*, I can quite confidently say that I'm sure that 'working more' has never been a regret of someone lying on their death bed. *I wish I worked more overtime hours, slept less, played more Angry Birds and generally, felt like I could stab my eyeballs out with a toothpick from stress overload*, **said no one ever**.

This raises the question. **Why work?** Gone are the days where ma & pa worked in order to bring home the bacon, *literally*. Working, and earning money, has expanded our purchasing capacity beyond simply putting food on the table. While many struggle to do just this, there are many who do so quite comfortably, and then have no idea what the hell they are doing with the rest of it. We now live in a day and age where we work in order to earn needless amounts of money to spend on supporting a particular lifestyle that's either energy intensive, earth degrading, money wasting, time consuming, meaningless or all of the above. I'm not one to come in and tell you how you should and shouldn't spend your money. What I want to do is to empower you to start thinking beyond your own self-determined rights and entitlements to that of your greater impact to the world around us and to sincerely ask yourself what living a rich life really means to you. We aren't merely 7 billion individuals living separately on this planet. Our lives are so intertwined, that one decision made by a person living on the other side of the planet has the potential to impact your life back home.

Some people work in order to earn enough money to send their children to college. Others work to create a safety net for their future life when they can no longer work. While there are others that work in order to pass the days (although I'm guessing these people may be few and far between). The problem is, many have no idea why they are *really* working. We do it because that's just what you do. All of these surface reasons come back to more deeper human needs like security, purpose, ambition, and happiness. Yet how much of the work that you do provides for these needs? Once you actually sit down and get an idea of exactly what you want to get from life and how much money you really need to cover your essential expenses, you may find yourself not needing to work quite as much as you think you do. Or freeing up the possibility to pursue a deeper passion. Imagine a life where you actually had the freedom and time to do more of the things that really bring these deeper desires into existence. Do you think working *more* is making it happen?

When we work mindlessly, we also are tempted to spend mindlessly because we have no purpose behind these practices. Possessions are merely a form of false riches that have us bound in shiny golden chains. The chains look pretty from the outskirts and my goodness, I'm sure some even envy them which is enough for most to let pride and peer approval fog their world view. When you are the one bound, the weight of these chains is more than unbearable at times. They merely hold us back, limiting our ability to enjoy life on an experiential and *experimental* level. It's a very simple equation. The more you have, the more risk there is in what you have to lose.

Ask yourself these questions. Have you ever turned down a weekend away or special occasions with loved ones because you have a mortgage to pay? Or thoughts of upgrading your car have taken priority over your next holiday? Maybe you've even turned down time with family because the house needs to be cleaned, or you needed to work an extra shift in order to pay off that long withstanding credit card debt. These 'adult responsibilities' need to be pulled back into perspective. Only you know the true state of your heart if you're being 100 percent honest with yourself.

The burdens of modern life are distracting you from living. They create an artificial dizziness that infiltrates and controls your subconscious. Sure, there will always be people out there who will use material splendor as a way to define success. You are not bound by their standards. Money can act as an enabler to do what you want when you want but it is not a metric. It's all about perception. As a society, we've collectively decided to adopt this form of exchange and place value on it. It has no value other than the value *you* place on it. Money is a tool that you can utilize to leverage these moments, but it in itself does not determine the outcome and it certainly can't buy everything. For one, you can't buy your way to happiness or a more sustainable life.

CHAPTER 9

Empower Yourself: The Crux of Your Choices

"Everyone has the right to live in a great place. More importantly, everyone has the right to contribute to making the place where they live already great."
- Fred Kent, Founder of 'Project for Public Spaces'

There was a time when I would stand at the checkout of a supermarket and look down at my basket of plastic wrapped groceries without a second thought. I would drive a measly mile down the road to the drive-thru of a certain fast food chain, just for a fifty-cent ice-cream cone. Then there were those times I would bask in a steamy hot shower in the middle of summer, feeling so overwhelmed by my day, I zoned out of life altogether for a whole precious thirty minutes as the wasted water drained away.

These are simple things that many give little thought to (I certainly didn't once upon an ignorant time) because singled out, **they seem harmless.** To multiply them by several thousand (or BILLION) and suddenly we have a grave situation of many, *many*, unconducive little habits on our hands. The magnitude of **you**, by way of the accumulation of your daily habits, **matter**.

"No snowflake in an avalanche ever feels responsible."
- Stanislaw Jerzy, Polish Poet

I was far from a perfect earthling but nor do I claim to be now. One thing I can say for sure is that my current lifestyle is leaps and bounds ahead of my days of young. I am not trying to 'up-stage' anyone or prove my 'greenness' over my neighbor. I am, however, out to improve on who I was yesterday, make better choices today and take responsibility for what happens tomorrow. This cannot be compared to your journey. What matters is that you are making the decision **to matter** and your choices reflect this attitude.

The accumulation of your choices is what has brought you to reading this book right now. There's power in this decision and I thank you for reading. But it's you who made that decision, *not me*. Not your mother, nor your father. No one else but you! In much the same way, it's the accumulation of our choices and actions that make up the change in this world. After all, corporations are made up of people sitting behind big desks. Governments are merely people in positions of power. Local and State councils are made up of people too. People with family and friends. People who will also be affected by the harrowing effects of climate change if we don't take steps now to make changes in our lifestyles today. One of my favorite quotes from the Dalai Lama is, *"If you think you are too small to make a difference, try sleeping with a mosquito."*

If you were to shower for 3 minutes as opposed to the average 10 minutes, you could be saving enough water to fill an Olympic swimming pool each year. In times of severe drought as we've witnessed recently in California and all over Australia and other parts of the world, that's significant water savings even if only one million people adopted this new lifestyle habit.

Forget about what other people are doing for the time being. Reclaim the power over your individual choices and control over your wallet. Don't carelessly throw money out at the latest and greatest because someone wants to push their product onto you without understanding who you are or what you want from life. You're better than that. *You're worth more than that.* When you are weighing up the decision on whether to buy the LG or the Samsung, question why you need to upgrade your television (or why you even need one in your life altogether). We are forever upgrading our lifestyles that otherwise serve no purpose other than to keep up with the latest technology and trends. Start re-framing your buying questions. What is it **costing** you and this planet to **not** have said product in your life? Is it worth your time, your money, the resources that are needed to produce it, and will it cost you more money down the track in the form of energy intensity and maintenance?

Let's back the truck up for a second and simplify what this might look like in everyday life. When you are standing there at the supermarket staring at the labels of two different packets of cereal, I challenge you to put them both back on the shelf and just walk away. While we can't all own acres of property to grow our own cereal crops, question whether it's an industry, a brand and a lifestyle that you want to support. The answers become simpler over time and you won't be standing there like a deer in headlights every time you need to make a purchasing decision about what to eat for breakfast. I'll elaborate more on this in the food section.

We want the best of both worlds but along the way, sacrifices need to be made. People just don't want to give up the supposed 'good life' even in the midst of denial that they are unhappier than ever. It's a freaking challenge to get out of this black hole of mental disillusion and one that takes constant reminders and practice. You will, *and I promise you this*, come to recognize these moments more and more as you practice sustainable living. In this consciousness you will be able to make the better choices whether for yourself or something bigger than yourself.

Your choices matter. Consider it an investment for your retirement fund. What lengths you go to now to reduce your carbon footprint will help you to better manage costs in the future. Pooled investments of many individuals act like a managed fund. Invested wisely, the dividends will show in the form of new job creation in a low-carbon economy that focuses on renewable energy, water conservation, organic food growing and land care. There's the potential for new opportunities in social growth and healthier people. In your own life, you'll reap the benefits of a lower cost of living immediately.

The European Union has released reports showing that increases in resource efficiency leads to job creation.[18] Countries in Northern Europe are already taking the lead in steering towards a greener economy. In Sweden, government initiatives that encourage eco-innovations have helped to boost job creation by 15 percent since 2007.[19] These are people leading by example rather than waiting on the side lines for the rest of the world to catch up. You needn't wait for permission from your government to start securing your own future if they are still behind the times. Follow the lead of those already walking on this path and know that you are not alone.

It's time to embrace the future and the need for sustainable lifestyle design not because we fear what's to come but because we want to preserve the things that we love about our current lifestyles. In order to do so, you need to understand what it is exactly you live for in life that makes you rich. What do you go to work for each day? What or whom are you making money for? What purpose does the money you earn serve in your own life? What gets you out of bed each morning? These are not meant to be rhetorical answers. I want you to answer them!

Do you make the choice now to start crafting yourself a sustainable lifestyle that's abundant in things that truly add value to life, or do you wait until you no longer have a choice? Are you an early adopter, a crowd follower, or a lagger? Do you wait until change is thrust upon you and you are left scrambling for some sense of semblance and meaning? Or do you act with intent and purpose now while you have the luxury to do so?

Whether you love to geek out about the science or not, we can all extract the natural by-products of a sustainable lifestyle. The riches of seeing that first seedling sprout in your backyard garden, the thrilling squeal of an excited child (or very mature adult) as they pick the first tomato from the vine, the feeling of satisfaction when a loved one comments you on a hearty home-cooked meal, the laughter of friends as you fumble over the dirt track hiking through the mountains, forgoing the annual 'spring clean' around the home in favour of a weekend away to spend time with the family because you no longer are cluttered by junk, and that priceless moment when you open your electricity bill to see it slashed to a few measly dollars.

The change is happening around you. It's already happening *inside* of you because you are here. And I am here. And we are having a conversation. **We need more conversations**. We need more education. We need more of this. In times when you feel your vote or voice does not count, remember the power of compounding choices.

The voice of a 13 year old girl from Grayslake, Illinois, was clearly enough to make waves in her community when she managed to rally over 174,000 supporters to sign her online petition for the Governor to veto a piece of legislation that would have prohibited towns in Illinois from enacting bans on single-use plastic bags. Yes, industry-backed lobbyists were trying to persuade politicians to ban the potential for bans on plastic bags. All it took was for a 13 year old and her army of backers, to stand up to them and now Illinois townships are even discussing banning single-use plastic bags for good.

> *"Never doubt that a small group of thoughtful, committed citizens can change the world; indeed, it's the only thing that ever has."*
> - Margaret Mead, Cultural Anthropologist

It matters when you care enough that you talk with others to educate them. They can in turn impact others. Within a year, the exponential potential is incredible. Dr Seuss says it best, *"Unless someone like you cares a whole awful lot, nothing is going to get better, it's not."*

CHAPTER 10

Finding Balance: Playing Limbo With Your Lifestyle

"Our personal consumer choices have ecological, social, and spiritual consequences. It is time to re-examine some of our deeply held notions that underlie our lifestyles."
- David Suzuki, Professor & Environmental Activist

Our modern lifestyles are grand. They are so super-sized beyond what's considered appropriate for our needs, that things once considered a luxury are the new norm in our ever revolving door of consumerism. With these blessings come great consequences though, and not all are for the betterment of man and dear Mother Nature.

With all the talk of healthy lifestyles across the media, blogosphere and vlogosphere, how many look beyond food and exercise? There are a lot of people out there who have spent far too long scrutinizing over the perfection of their diet and exercise regimes, they forget to look beyond and see that there are other parts of their lifestyles that are keeping them from feeling whole. You can eat the 'cleanest' foods and exercise until the body-builders come home, but all this accounts for nothing at the end of the day if the earth is in ruins around you.

If you think all there is to leading a balanced and healthy lifestyle is making sure you drink your green juice each day, then think again. Let's consider it in a more holistic view then, shall we? *That seems to be all the rage these days.*

Lifestyle encompasses so much more than simply what we eat and how we exercise. It covers a broad spectrum of areas in life from diet to exercise, hobbies, work, spirituality, family and social relationships. Your consumptive habits, daily routines and mental attitudes; these all influence the complete package.

We have warped expectations as to what goes into maintaining these healthy lifestyles that we so desperately want to lead. We expect organic bananas all year round. Yet how many people live in regions where this is viable without the draining reliance on fuel hungry transportation to get it there? How many people participate in the process of bringing food to their plate? We expect cell phone upgrades every twelve months. Yet we complain about our monthly phone bills and have a nice collection of iPhones building up. New shoes each season. Though how dare you suggest I spend more money on sustainable, pasture raised eggs. For the shops to be open 24/7. But don't dare come knocking on your door when a neighbor is in need. This is all sounds reasonable, *right*? If using the measuring stick of modern expectations, then of course it does. We demand the best, the biggest and the fastest at the cheapest prices - **now**. These are the expectations instilled upon us through our modern lifestyles.

But since when were these conducive to a life beyond yours?

The fact of the matter is this; we need to adjust our lenses through which we see the world. To see change in this world, you have to be the change. Only you can determine your course of action and reaction. You have as much chance in directly impacting the course of humankind and our consequential impact on this planet by addressing your own lifestyle *first*. I'm not here to dissuade anyone from striving for front row seat in senate because earth knows how desperately we need better policy-makers in such positions. What I implore you to do is to first evaluate your own lifestyle before jumping down the throat of another. For how can we help others if we first don't understand the nature of our own lifestyles? At the end of the day, we really only have the power over our own decisions but it's through these that we can be catalysts for change in the world around us.

CHAPTER 11

A New Lifestyle Code

"We cannot hope to create a sustainable culture with any but sustainable souls."
- Derrick Jensen, Author of 'Endgame, Vol. 1: The Problem of Civilization'

A sustainable lifestyle is more than putting an empty milk carton in the recycling bin, drinking green smoothies or purchasing eco-friendly toothbrushes. *It's a way of life.* You need to dig deeper here than the mainstream notion of sustainability that has sadly become 'green-washed'. We want to do more than preach superficial 'green' initiatives with little practice and substance to follow it up. It's one thing to walk around wearing a T-shirt declaring your love for the pastime of tree-hugging and another thing altogether to be out there planting those trees. *Although I will always support a good tree hugging session*, if we are going to be real activists, then **action** is required.

"It's about what we can do and want to do, rather than what we oppose and want others to change."
- David Holmgren, Permaculture Practitioner

You can make a positive contribution with limited time and resources by *just starting with something* to role-model what that change looks like. This kind of revolution starts with the people. That is, you and I. **This is our call to action.**

These following five principles of Sustainable Lifestyle Design exist to provoke thought, to inspire change and instigate a shift from an attitude of problem-probing, to solution-seeking.

1. **To Give Back to the Earth**

2. **To Reduce Your Eco-Footprint**

3. **To Promote Health and Wellness**

4. **To Share With the Community**

5. **To Live Freely and Abundantly**

We'll delve deeper into each of these principles in the following chapters. A sustainable lifestyle promotes and supports health and wellness in all facets of your life whilst nurturing the environment around you. It has a positive influence on the world because it naturally reduces your carbon footprint. Your senses awaken as you experience a richer planet. It's authentic. It's real. It's practical. It's about balance. It doesn't require you to live beyond your means; mentally, physically, emotionally or financially. **It just makes sense**.

PART 3

PRINCIPLE 1
TO GIVE BACK TO THE EARTH

CHAPTER 12

The Gift of Giving Back

"Nature is inexhaustibly sustainable if we care for it. It is our universal responsibility to pass a healthy earth onto future generations."
- Sylvia Dolson, Author of 'Joy of Bears'

Ownership is an intriguing idea. Who decided the land you stand on is yours to own? It's one thing to own the rights to a piece of property, but another thing entirely to do as you wish with it. Where do you draw the line between earth degrading practices that show a complete and utter disregard for Mother Nature's right to *her* property? This notion that we can freely extract the natural resources of the land *at her cost*, and claim them as our own in an unjust manner is driving us to the brink of self-destruction.

Many indigenous cultures did not possess this same idea of property ownership. They didn't consider themselves as rulers who were out to conquer, plunder and own. They were as much a part of the land as the birds, the wildebeest and the plants. **We are no different.**

We live in a different era where property rights are a tangible thing because a piece of paper says so. This does **not** give us permission to disregard our responsibility to the earth beneath our feet.

When we extract from the earth through agriculture and the gathering of natural resources, we take the very energy from Mother Earth that she accumulated over many generations. This 'energy' isn't a new age, voodoo, *call on the spirits from the underworld* concept either. We extract generations of biomass accumulated in earth's soil whether we harvest grown food or knock down an ancient forest. Multitudes of plant materials, animals, insects and micro-organisms have died, decayed and degraded in order to provide food for new life in what 'The Lion King' has taught us is referred to as, *"The Circle of Life."* Without death there can be no life. Mother Nature is not wasteful in this process. She utilizes every single last piece of energy possible to generate new life so that we can go on living. Take a moment to give thanks for this process. It's a precious and humbling cycle that we need to remind ourselves is *natural* and one we ourselves are part of.

This natural cycle subsequently *recycles* these nutrients back into the soil and into the food we eat. This layer of rich, dark, organic topsoil is otherwise known as "humus." It's soil that is alive and brimming with micro-life from the decayed and decomposed materials of their forefathers; creating substance for new life. The more nutrient dense and mineral rich humus is, the more nutrient dense and mineral rich our food will be. **We should treat this resource like precious gold.** Sadly, over the course of human existence, specifically since the introduction of agriculture, two-thirds of the world's humus has been depleted. We can actively participate in the rebuilding of humus by acts of intention every day.

Here's 3 things you can do:

1. Compost

Most by-products from the kitchen have organic value and can be recycled through composting for use in the garden. These may include everyday household waste items like your kitchen scraps (peels, skin, cores, coffee grounds), garden matter (grass clippings, dry leaves, small twigs), herbivore and chicken manure, shredded paper and cardboard (non-glossy and non-treated). If you live in the city and are unable to maintain your own compost heap, think of participating in some alternatives that I have outlined as a free downloadable guide on my blog.

2. Start a Worm Farm

Worms are some of the hardest and most effective workers you can employee to recycle nutrients back into your gardening system and the earth. Whether you have just a few container herbs or a thriving food forest, by utilizing the 'worm castings' (aka, worm juice) from a worm farm, you have created your own organic, liquid fertilizer. No chemicals needed! I'll speak more on my favorite little creatures in a later chapter.

You can easily build your own worm farm or if that doesn't peak your interest, they're available from most good hardware and gardening stores or online. I have instructions on my website that detail how to make one using recycled materials. If worms make you squirm, there's an alternative called a Bokashi Composting System that's perfect for indoor environments. More information has been included in my resources section at the back of this book.

3. Grow Your Own Food

Gardening is an opportunity to connect with Mother Nature; a chance to learn from her many years of experience and if managed properly, within which we can also give back to the earth more than we take. Through the act of gardening, we practice the precious skills of patience, management and stewardship. Tend to your garden with care and kindness and in return, it will bless you with an abundance of organic and healthy food. Too many people blindly follow the conventional wisdom of yesterday that espouses nature-destroying, not nature-restoring gardening techniques. A fantastic resource on growing your own organic food to utilize natural biomass can be found in the resource section.

If you're only starting out with growing food, focus on high value varieties that make sense for your local climate. For example, buying fresh herbs each week easily adds up to a few hundred dollars a year. It's cost effective to grow your own (in containers if you have limited space) that provide you with a continual supply.

CHAPTER 13

Recycling The Sexy Back Into Soil

"I can't imagine anything more important than air, water, soil, energy and biodiversity. These are the things that keep us alive."
- David Suzuki, Founder of The David Suzuki Foundation

The soil of this planet is akin to the digestive health of our guts; a place where bacteria both good and bad have the opportunity to flourish, depending on the conditions. An imbalanced system shows through disease, pathogens, pests, and the quality of food you are able (or unable) to produce. Chemical pesticides, herbicides and fungicides are akin to antibiotics. In targeting the "culprit" or pathogens, they also strip the soil of good bacteria and fungi necessary to creating a healthy environment for plants to grow in. You are undoing the years of hard work Mother Nature has spent accumulating rich nutrients in the soil and a thriving ecosystem for her micro-organisms. Conventional gardening techniques would see to you replacing these lost nutrients by utilizing synthetic fertilizers. It's a codependent cycle. Manufacturing synthetic chemicals and fertilizers in an attempt to undo the damage rather than practicing more holistic gardening techniques is an unsustainable practice. It's also one big money-flogging exercise.

Why spend hundreds (if not thousands) of dollars on these products and killing off any long-term opportunity you have of maintaining a self-sustainable ecosystem to grow food within when Mother Nature is well equipped to deal with this process. You just need to practice the nurturing role of stewardship in managing the process. No PHD in horticulture required. *Thank goodness.*

It's become a sad reflection on society that growing food is something we 'advance' from in stepping towards the technological era when the cultivation of food is the fundamental basis of society. Where do you think our food will come from in the future if we do not participate in protecting the very little healthy soil we have left on this planet? Let's give back some respect that is deserved to the food growers of this world!

We cannot eat good food that is healthful for us unless we help sustain a healthful planet. One with clean air and water, nutrient rich soil and biodiversity in both flora and fauna to maintain a balanced ecosystem. Mother Nature loves homoeostasis as much as our bodies do. We cannot maintain our diets and lifestyles for optimal wellness unless we first, care for this planet. In working through Principle 1 - **To Give back to the Earth**, we are continuously looking for ways to be earth *regenerators*, not *degenerators*. Let's not consider ourselves as merely conservationists but rather, active 'regenerationists' of Mother Nature and her soil.

CHAPTER 14

Dirty Dancing and Doing the Worm

"Earthworms will dance."
-Joel Salatin, Sustainable Farmer

The award for most unappreciated creature on this planet *must* go to the humble earthworm. Their ability to take our kitchen scraps, coffee grounds, organic waste, recycled papers, *you name it*, and churn them into energy we in turn use for growing more food is possibly the most efficient and inspiring biological process. They are real life superheros *dude*. They inject life into soil. Talk about superpowers. As worthy of a Nobel Peace prize as they are, they can't take all the credit of course. Help comes to them in the form of their trusty sidekicks; micro-organisms. Together though, **they are a force to be reckoned with.**

The earthworm is a turbo-charged eating, composting and pooping machine. Programmed to be the ultimate burrower, it's role in maintaining soil health cannot be understated. They aerate the soil (keeping it from becoming compacted and break it up if it is), improve its water holding capacity, create fertile channels that allow plant root systems to find a home, neutralise soil that is too acidic or alkaline, digest and liberate essential nutrients into a usable form of food for plants and micro-organisms and let's just conclude, *basically hold the whole entire planet together.* A round of applause please!

They are the ultimate genderless species, opting to reproduce with whoever looks sexy that day providing the conditions are right for them to do so. Give them some mood lighting, cool temperatures, a moist bed, and you have a night to be remembered. So remember this when preparing a home for you new favorite pet.

Scientists estimate there are over 4000 species of earthworm. They can roughly be broken in three subcategories, each playing a specific role in maintaining our soil's health. There are the deep burrowers who prefer to dig horizontally, the middle dwellers designed to burrow vertically and the kind that you will be more concerned with; the earthworms living in the topsoil which will find their way into open compost bins (do note that only specific breeds of worms are suitable for enclosed worm farms). They are resilient to changing conditions and prefer to live in close quarters to each other; *Brady Bunch style*.

The survival of our species is dependent on maintaining the integrity of our soil. On a home-scale, we can utilize the composting process to foster a healthy environment conducive to supporting this micro-ecosystem beneath our feet. Composting uses local resources, recycles your food waste, reduces landfill and negates your dependence on synthetic fertilizers. Your life depends on worms and micro-organisms. NOT some super techno-machine that will somehow, magically continue to pump an infinite supply of fertilizer sourced from the depths of the galaxy. Stop punishing these creatures by contaminating the soil with your assortment of atomic gardening products.

As mentioned earlier, we can relate the soil's ecosystem to the inner-workings of our own digestive systems. Maintaining balanced micro-flora in our gut allows us to effectively and efficiently absorb nutrients so we can thrive in good health. The soil's ecosystem acts in a similar manner. This can be achieved *organically* of course. As a healthy and probiotic-rich gut can ward off illness in our own bodies, so too can a healthy, balanced, and life abundant soil ward off pests and disease.

When we rip up our soils (yes, I'm talking about plowing and tillage), whether on the grand scale as seen in industrial agriculture or even in your own backyard, you disturb this delicate ecosystem. Rather than knocking on the door, you are storming right on in as an uninvited guest, wreaking havoc on the micro-ecosystem beneath. Ripping up annual crops and tilling soil every season, releases unnecessary carbon into the atmosphere. This also requires more energy input from you as the gardener as it speeds up the process of nutrient release. While this may sound like a good thing, it actually overloads the plants with *too* many nutrients in the short term and much of the excess is washed away when the next rains come. Further inputs will be required to re-inject these nutrients that were lost. This is a fundamental problem with industrial agriculture. It's not that the plants don't receive enough nutrients through synthetic fertilizers, it's that they receive *too much, too fast* and the excess nitrogen run-off is contaminating the waterways and disturbing ecosystems outside of the farming zone.

The process of tilling is akin to peeling back the skin of the earth. Ouch! Think of it as your own skin. Dare I say again, we are products of nature and our biology is replicated from what we see in Mother Nature. The thought of scratching at it and tearing it up is like a Freddy Kruger nightmare coming to life. The same principles can be applied to how we treat the earth. That's why more and more research and support is being poured into no-till farming and gardening methods.

On a home-scale, you can minimize the disturbance of your garden beds through good design to allow easy access and walkways that don't interfere with the growing area. Growing more perennial plants (which produce and reseed on their own accord for years on end) encourages a mature soil system as they can go undisturbed for years. Keep your soil well mulched to hold moisture and encourage earthworms to do their job of aerating the soil. Investing the time and effort into building your own worm farm (or buying one), will give you access to an endless supply of home-brewed, organic fertilizer. There are other methods you can incorporate to promote soil health too, such as chopping and dropping plants when pruning, planting nitrogen fixing plants, avoiding synthetic chemicals and planting cover crops between rotations. These methods are too detailed and vast to cover in great depth in this book but there are entire books you'll find dedicated to the individual topics and I'll reference some in the resources section.

Think through the process of cattle grazing and you'll come to understand why so many applaud these initiatives of rotational grassland farming as an earth regenerative practice. Cattle are beneficial for soil restoration because, when managed properly, they provide nitrogen through their patties and don't tear up the grass but 'trim' it as one would shave or trim their facial hair. Not ripping it up like one would wax hair on your legs. Yeah, *that freaking hurts*.

Each time you harvest plants, you are taking some of those nutrients from the soil. We are always talking about giving back to Mother Nature more than we take. It's important to replace those lost nutrients to maintain a healthy balance in your soil. Over time, you will begin to rebuild the soil integrity and this is one of the greatest investments you can make for yourself, the planet and future generations. It's time to whip out the dirty dancing, reconnect with your garden, and get your worm on!

PART 4

PRINCIPLE 2
TO REDUCE YOUR ECO-FOOTPRINT

CHAPTER 15

The Low Carbon Diet

"Treat the Earth well. It was not given to you by your parents. It was loaned to you by your children."
- Kenyan Proverb

We are facing a global crisis of unprecedented levels. Our population is set to explode in the coming 50 years to 9 billion. With the advent of mass scale agriculture during the 1950s, otherwise unfortunately and misleadingly, widely referred to as the 'green revolution', our global population has dramatically swelled in a shockingly short period. During the 20th century alone, it's grown from 1.65 billion to 6 billion. *Industrialization has enabled us to breed like rabbits.*

It's hard to imagine, at the rate we are going now, how we can sustain our current, energy greedy lifestyles, when millions go without food, shelter, clothes, and even clean water each day. While there are also deeper seeded blockades inhibiting positive changes for a majority of the world's most impoverished nations, such as political corruption, unequal distribution of goods and services, as well as human rights injustices, we still have a responsibility to mitigate our own carbon footprint.

Roughly 80% of the world's energy is being consumed by only 20% of the world's population. If you are a citizen of the USA, Australia, Canada, UK, some European countries, and the wealthy upper class in general, you are likely part of that number.

Too often we find ourselves fixated on controlling uncontrollable variables when our efforts are better exerted changing the course of our own lives. It's time to focus on the BIG wins that make a significant impact on your eco-footprint. Forgoing the use of plastic bags will only go so far if the rest of your lifestyle doesn't exemplify these good intentions.

1. Buy locally grown produce

Bypass the supermarkets that are more often than not, hubs for low-quality, cheap, and unsustainably produced imported food from all the exploited corners of the globe and leaves local farmers with little more than a cent to their name. This dependence on external, uncontrollable variables have paved the way for an unsustainable food system. This involves high transport costs, a dependence on conventional agriculture which utilizes earth-degrading chemicals in their processes, and stockpiling obese profits among a select few multinational corporations. It doesn't paint a favorable picture. You really are voting with your dollar every time you choose to buy locally and support farmers doing the right thing. Local farmers' markets or Community Supported Agriculture (CSA) programs are a good starting point.

2. Understand who & what you are financially investing in

Where you invest your money is as crucial as what you are spending your disposable consumer dollar on. There are growing opportunities surrounding ethical investments, credit unions and local co-op businesses. Entrepreneurs now have such widespread access to peer funding through online platforms like Kickstarter and Indiegogo. It's eliminated the previously high barriers of entry to many marketplaces. You needn't look far to find a clever bunch of people striving to inspire the world with their passion and get you on board.

If you want to take power back from corporations you morally disagree with, invest your money elsewhere. Support initiatives that invest in regenerative agriculture, forest restoration, renewable energy and sustainable community development. These things are the way of the future whether Wall Street forecasts otherwise or not.

3. Seek alternative methods for consuming goods

Buy second hand, borrow or trade where possible. There are local second-hand charity stores in almost every city. My favorite websites for second-hand goods include Craigslist, Gumtree, Ebay and Freecycle. Need a slow cooker? Can you begin to imagine the number of wedding gifted slow cookers that remain unopened. I scored one off Ebay for $10. Need a drill for a weekend DIY project? Ask the neighbor rather than buying one brand new that you will never use again. You'll save yourself some money in the process. Recycle or bring to life goods that still have another life left in them. Give that wobbly coffee table some TLC and you'll have a whole new piece of furniture that will give IKEA a run for its money. How about trading your backyard grown veggies with neighbors in exchange for other food or services? You don't need to be victim to this endless pursuit of mind-numbing entertainment and consumption!

4. Reduce your electricity usage

Electricity remains the single-largest source of CO_2 emissions from energy, with 11.7 billion tonnes of CO_2 released in 2010.[20] Your first call-to-action should be to understand just how much energy you consume. Look at your past electricity bills and consider purchasing a low-cost home energy-monitoring device. These devices measure energy usage and can give you an estimation of greenhouse gas emissions. This will set you a baseline of your consumption and provide real-time feedback which encourages behavioural change.

Solar energy is one of the most abundant forms of renewable energy available to man. Given the right circumstances, it can result in significant cost and energy savings over the long term. A solar panel installation can, however, be a large expense upfront and may not make sense for everyone's situation but in sunny geographical regions like where I am in Brisbane, Australia, solar power makes both long term financial and environmental sense. A household solar system can save 35,180 pounds of carbon dioxide per year. It's well documented the long term savings are enough to offset the upfront costs given the average guarantee of a solar installation is 20 - 25 years. An Australian case study explains, *"If a 2kW system costs around $5000 to install and cuts 30 percent from your power bill, you would be saving around $150 each quarter on a $500 bill. It would take you around 8 years (34 quarters) to pay off this installation."*[21]

Some companies offer leasing options if the upfront cost is too much. In America, if you've ever considered the option, the time to install solar panels is now. The federal solar Investment Tax Credit (ITC) offers a 30 percent tax credit for residential and commercial properties that convert to solar energy by the end of 2016. Check with your local councils to see what rebate programs are available and if you can apply. Here's some further ideas to help you save money and reduce your electricity costs around the home.

- Line dry your clothes. Driers are energy hungry machines.

- Turn your computer and other large electrical appliances off at the power outlet when not in use (especially when you go on vacation).

- Utilize natural sunlight during the day, not indoor lighting.

- Get rid of those incandescent light bulbs as soon as possible and opt for energy saving LED ones.

- Invest in proper insulation for your home, seal draughts and/or get double-glazing on your windows. These things help to reduce your need for electric heating and cooling.

5. Be water smart

Fresh and accessible clean water makes up only one percent of total water on this planet. Water pollution is a vivid threat to this precious and limited water supply. A Unesco report states, *"Some 2 million tons of waste per day are disposed of within receiving waters, including industrial wastes and chemicals, human waste and agricultural wastes (fertilizers, pesticides and pesticide residues)."*[22] The average household wastes a staggering 121 liters (30 gallons) of water a day.[23] It's a startling realization that we need to treat this resource with the same consideration we give money. By implementing even just a few of the below suggestions will significantly cut your wastage.

- A rainwater harvesting tank is a simple solution for most households to capture and recycle rainwater. I know in some parts of the world, like Colorado, it is illegal so speak with your local council first. The appropriate sized tank to meet your needs will be determined by annual average rainfall for your area, how much water catchment your roof can provide and the available space you have to situate the storage tank. Often the average household can get away with a 9000 liter (1500 gallon) tank to tie them over between rainfalls. A local specialist will be able to advise you further.

- Install a greywater system that recycles waste-water from bathroom sinks and laundry machines for outdoor watering. The water is filtered, either through natural garden design (such as a small swamp and pond) or artificial means to make it safe for use in the garden. Using biodegradable and natural products in your home reduces the intensity of this process.

- A low-flow shower-head attachment can be bought for a few dollars and reduces the amount of water being used per shower by almost half. It personally saves us upwards of $300 a year off our water bill.

- Combine this with the water savings from installing a dual-flush toilet (or the cheaper option, by placing something like a filled water bottle into the toilet cistern) and you're looking at some nice piggy-bank money.

- Wash your clothes in cold water and only if you have a full load. This is more energy efficient than hot washes and does not ruin clothes in the same way hot water washing does. The only instance hot water should be used is if you have a full load and your clothes are extra soiled.

- You can also conserve water usage by turning off the tap when brushing your teeth, washing dishes, shampooing your hair and shaving.

- Avoid unnecessarily washing your car and polluting the waterways with harsh chemicals.

- Watering plants at dawn or dusk and using garden mulch also reduces the amount of water being evaporated and wasted.

- Healthy, well nourished soil in the garden acts as a sponge and naturally retains water and minimizes run-off.

6. Cut transport energy use

If you're always the one complaining about how much money you forked out on car expenses, look at the car you drive. Can you downsize to a more economical vehicle or forgo a car altogether? A fuel-guzzling SUV in the city is unnecessary. Cars account for the second largest household expense after mortgage or rent payments. I'm not calling on you to go out and buy a brand new hybrid. We can't all afford a Prius and nor are you socially superior if you do. Wearing environmental social badges doesn't win anyone brownie points if the rest of your lifestyle is in shambles.

If you can't walk, bicycle, catch public transport or car pool (another perfect example of where pooled resources provides a greater energy efficiency), only then should you use your own personal vehicle.

7. Become a Homesteading Guru

Time to bust out those 'Great Depression' glass jars and get preserving, culturing, pickling, you name it. Not only are fermented and cultured foods amazing for your health by encouraging beneficial gut bacteria, they are a great way to utilize vegetables that need to be used. My two favorite staples are sauerkraut and milk kefir which are so simple to make. You can get the recipes here and here.

We've lost touch with these age old traditions and it's about time we dug them up again so our children have a chance at learning the importance of self-sustenance. DIY clothes, cleaning products, furniture, decorations, gifts - let your imagination run wild! *Or just refer to Google and Youtube.* Self-sufficiency is not a sign of deprivation. It signals pro-activeness and frugality, making way for abundance within other areas of your life.

8. Cut the plastic and packaging

Did you know that plastic bags take centuries to degrade? Every single plastic bag ever created is still in existence today! For all the convenience they appear to offer, they contribute to the greatest environmental problems faced by man; pollution, killing wildlife, dependence on non-renewable resources like oil and contributing to toxic leaching of non-biodegradable landfill. Decline plastic shopping bags at the checkout. Carry your reusable bags with you or ask to use a recyclable cardboard box instead. Opt for minimal packaging wherever possible. Pack lunches and leftovers in washable stainless steel or glass containers that will last for years. Say no to plastic in whatever shape or form it comes in *wherever possible.* Be a plastic police!

9. Eliminate the toxic chemicals

Now I'm not here to fear-monger you into writing off every single chemical in a glazing generalization as being evil. 'Chemicals' after all, can be both synthetic or organic in nature. Both good or bad for our health. I don't even have a chemistry background to understand this. What I do not advocate though, is deliberately drenching ourselves in copious amounts of toxic synthetic chemicals as we do each and every single day, and then eating them as well to top it all off. Not when there are perfectly healthy and beneficial natural alternatives available.

Think about this (in fact, do this!). If you were to read the labels of all these products that most people use on a daily basis, you will walk away with a list longer than a seven year old's wish list for Santa. I'll take a guess the number is in the hundreds. Your shampoo, face cleanser, hand soap, clothes washing powder, dish washing detergent, the sprays on the food you eat, the ingredients in the food you eat, car fumes you breathe in, home cleaning products, beauty cosmetics, sunscreens... they're all loaded. Many of the ingredients in these products are not only harming your own health, but being washed out to the environment, putrefying our waterways and intoxicating our soil. You might ask, why are they allowed to be sold to us then and even deemed 'safe'? Although you should also note the number that have warning labels.

Single handed, no one chemical on its own is going to bring down the fate of mankind, *unless it's uranium in the form of a nuclear warhead or too much carbon in the atmosphere* (oh wait, we're slowly getting to that point). It's the conglomeration of these ingredients that add up, and in time, are being stored in the very walls of our cells and the cells of the earth that create a toxic environment for life. The effects are only beginning to unfold in the form of allergies, skin disorders and yes, even the big 'C' – Cancer. Many of these potions and concoctions are relatively new to our species. Sure, we're a hardy bunch who are highly adaptable to changing environments and our bodies have a magnificent natural mechanism for detoxing but this load we're putting on it further, it's unnecessary. We may not be morphing into mutated three armed, googly-eyed monsters overnight but a flare up of inflamed skin in response to using a commercial face cleanser that's supposedly 'safe,' is enough to raise the alarm bells. We're inflicting unnecessary stress onto the detoxification pathways of our bodies.

Just because a label has "organic" or "natural" scribbled all over, does not mean it's good for you or the environment. Many products are 'naturally' derived but the process they've gone through, and the synthetic fillers that have been added, do little to support that title. If you can find an authentically natural and organic brand you trust and want to support, that's great. Being the frugalist I am though, I encourage you to experiment with making your own. Here's a little recipe for an all-purpose home cleaner to get you started. I recommend using any of the following ingredients:

White Vinegar: *Cuts grease, disinfects and deodorizes*

Baking Soda: *Neutralizes smells, lifts dirt and whitens*

Castile Soap: *Lifts dirt and cuts grease*

Lemon: *Disinfects and smells amazing*

Essential Oils: Deodorizes and disinfects (e.g. lavender, tea tree oil, eucalyptus)

Here's an example:

- ½ cup distilled white vinegar

- 6 drops essential oil of your choice

Add water to fill the remaining and shake ingredients together in a spray bottle.

10. Energy-star ratings matter

If you need to upgrade an old appliance, like an irreparable broken washing machine, it's a financial investment to choose a model with a five star energy rating. Energy ratings are government regulated and can result in hundreds, if not thousands of dollars, in cost savings over the life of the machine.

11. Don't spend beyond your means

When you buy beyond your means, you set yourself up for a financial and energy-sucking burden in the future. Unutilized space costs you time, money and energy. A house of three empty bedrooms still requires cleaning and maintenance. If not managed properly, you could even be unnecessarily heating or cooling them. Then there's the cost of paying a mortgage for an unutilized space.

This rule of thumb can be applied to all areas of life. The bigger the car, fridge, house, property, wardrobe, you name it, the more expensive it will be. Unless of course, you utilize them efficiently. If you live on an acre property and cultivate an abundance of food, then that's awesome. Growing up in a family of eight, we utilized the same space as a family of three. I still wonder how my parents managed on a single income and while they barely did, I'm here now, alive and well. We were happy and healthy children. Sure, sharing a room with my sister was less than optimal at times, but certainly far more efficient and a great incentive for me to leave the nest when I was able. Yet families on a double income trying to maintain a lifestyle made up of inefficient energy sucking habits and grand mansions is nonsense. Living within your means is not deprivation. It's rational and logical.

12. Family plan if you plan to have children

While we may never face a one child policy mandated by government as witnessed in China, we can be intentional about family planning. As every couple should have a right to express their human instincts to breed, as should every child have the right to be brought into the world under the loving care of parents in a stable and nurturing environment. Sadly, we know this not to be the case. While bigger issues are being played out here, like access to education and the availability of contraception to those who need it most, we all still have a part to play. Thoughtfully planned pregnancies, using contraception or even providing a home for an orphan or foster child are issues that need more public discussion.

13. Be conscious of your consumptive patterns

Your eco-footprint is a reflection of your life values. The more grand and extreme your consumptive patterns are, the less room you have for other things in your life. Furthermore, the greater your carbon footprint, the more effort (and often money) is required to minimize it. There is no shame in making the intentional decision to downsize your lifestyle if your current income (or mental capacity) can not support it. This takes courage in a world that values material possessions over human sanity. Insanity would be trying to maintain an unsustainable image all in the name of false ideals or invisible social pressures. If you can't keep up with your credit card debt, cut the ties it has over your life. Get serious about budgeting. Downsize the home, the car, the fashion addiction, the excessive entertainment expenses, the unhealthy eating, drinking and smoking habits. Yes, 'sacrifices' need to be made but no sooner will you realize the absence of these things will open space for more important things in life. Like pursuing sidelined hobbies, rekindling relationships and the all important 'time' so many of us complain about not having enough of.

A sustainable lifestyle is not about deprivation. It's about carefully and intentionally selecting how you invest your time and money. What we learn from this mentality is that in time, we gain clarity to what we truly value in life and begin to see *things* for they really are; merely *things* we assign a certain level of value to. When we are so overwhelmed by the physical and mental clutter in our lives, we find ourselves in a position where even the presence of these 'things' no longer bring us comfort or joy. Does it make sense now why a life of 'less' creates space for *more*?

Thinking in this way allows you to make conscious decisions about consuming what *adds* value to your life rather than things that *take away from it*. This is not limited to tangible goods either. Just like in the food you eat and the people you hang around with, you are the product of the information you consume. On a daily basis we are exposed to hundreds, if not thousands, of mixed messages from advertisements, news reports, websites, other people's opinions – it's overwhelming! Everyone is trying to sell you a product, an idea or their opinion and this in itself is not the problem. The problem is how you perceive the situation, how effective your internal filtering system is and how you respond.

When you immerse yourself in the gossip columns, read the global news first thing when you wake up, stress over the falling stock market, and gawk at depressing images of the latest neighborhood shootings, your internal stress signals go haywire! These things affect you on a subconscious and physiological level. What's the point if we're all walking around like a bunch of over-stressed, over-worked, depressed, sick and insane zombies? There are more effective ways we can support those in need that doesn't involve you sacrificing your sanity. You can be an informed citizen of this world but without the need to consume low quality information.

This 'need' to be connected and wired 24/7 is a modern day phenomena and an addiction in itself. When you make decisions stemming from this '*fear of missing out*' syndrome, you are not acting in your best interests. When you act from a place of fear, this will affect your experiences negatively. Whether it be a fear of fat, fear of climate change, fear of failure or fear of being alone. It may be fear initially that catches your attention but it's through love, understanding and a desire to do better for ourselves and the world that creates the long term change.

Try doing a "news fast", a "gossip fast" or a "social media fast" for a week and see how this impacts your time, your interactions with the outside world and the conversations with those around you. Shrink your sphere of concern to what you *can* influence in your immediate life, given your circumstances. After this initial week, you may wish to slowly start filtering in more positive influences, messages of empowerment and people who are leading the lifestyle that you want to live. Periodically it helps to go back and do a 'detox' of these information streams to see what no longer serves you.

CHAPTER 16

The Food Pyramid of a Sick Society

"Asking the Department of Agriculture to promote healthy eating was like asking Jack Daniels to promote responsible drinking."
- Denise Minger, Author of 'Death by Food Pyramid'

The standard Western diet is dominated by highly processed and packaged food; factory farmed meats, cheap and low quality imitation products (such as margarine), low fat (aka high sugar) deceptions, rancid refined seed oils (canola, vegetable, soy) fluorescent orange cheese, watered-down skim milk (you're being ripped off), and **fortified** grains and cereals for good measure. *We don't want you lacking in vital nutrients now.* At what point in human history did food need to be artificially fortified with extra nutrients anyway? Such as the white bread "fortified with vitamin B" and the watery milk fortified with "extra calcium." Somewhere lost in between are a few measly servings of fruits and vegetables, probably hidden within a microwavable meal or "fruit" muesli bar. *Healthy is certainly not a word that comes to mind.* And yet these are Government recommendations forming the basis of the western food pyramid and widely supported by charitable 'health' institutions like The Heart Foundation. The same institutions that are suppose to have your best health interests at heart but will shut the door on you if the back door is being knocked on by a food manufacturing company with a wad of cash in their briefcase. I call bogus on this one as to who it's really benefiting. You're allowed to be skeptical and ask questions. **It's your health at stake here.**

Every nutrient we need is available for consumption in nature. It's what man has done to degrade the quality of these nutrients wherein lies the problem. We process, refine and heat the life out it and expect to get the same results. *I think not bullseye.*

The food manufacturing industry is banking on the hope that consumers remain uneducated and feeling dispirited to make better decisions for the sake of their health and the planet. That's not to say that there isn't a time and place for these things but in our *daily* life? Certainly not. Coupled with the diet industry, they are often washed with advertising of false hopes and promises. Making money off our sickness and despair. Real food eating is not a fad diet. It's eating as nature intended man to eat and it's in our best interests to do so. We'll get into what that looks like soon.

There are, of course, the minority with good intentions who are doing great things for the advancement of human health. Unfortunately, they are just that; *the minority.* What you can do today is to empower and educate yourself to become a master of your own health through diet and lifestyle; the greatest form of preventative medicine. The measures you go to now to invest in your own wellness will minimize your potential reliance on an overburdened medical industry in years to come.

CHAPTER 17

Why Eating Everything on Your Plate Won't Solve World Hunger

"If we grew our own food, we wouldn't waste a third of it as we do today. If we made our own tables and chairs, we wouldn't throw them out the moment we changed the interior décor. If we had to clean our own drinking water, we probably wouldn't shit in it."
- Mark Boyle, Author of 'The Moneyless Manifesto'

When we talk about world hunger, **food scarcity is not the problem**. One out of every three calories produced globally are never eaten, which isn't just a waste of food but of water, land and energy.[24] We have a problem here that's due to negative lifestyle habits and wasteful supply chain management practices. The nutritional quality of what we are dedicating our resources towards producing and the consequential distribution of that food to those who need it most has been misdirected.

For a majority of us, we grew up being ordered to eat everything on our plate, Brussels sprouts and all. Or *we'd risk being looked down upon unfavorably by the dessert gods.* This mentality, *whilst full of good intentions I'm sure ma & pa*, is not necessarily doing anyone any good. That's right, it's not reducing our food wastage or helping to promote a healthy relationship with food. It's having the reverse effect. Sorry mother, but eating that last carrot on my plate will not save a starving child in Africa. Lucky for her and for me, I love my carrots!

Studies have shown that children forced to eat everything in front of them lost the ability to know when to stop eating and those denied certain foods were likely to compensate by eating unhealthy foods elsewhere.[25] By encouraging children to *'rely on environmental indicators, like how much food is on their plates or the time of day, they'll lose the ability to rely on internal cues to know whether they're hungry or full.'*[26] Couple this with our increasing portion sizes of Western diets and what **kinds of food** make up the average family's dinner plate (deep fried fish fingers and chips anyone?) and you are setting your children up for a future of disordered eating. *If only it were Brussels sprouts and broccoli they were actually being asked to eat.*

The underpinning psychological effects this has on us as we grow older is just one more reason why we struggle as a society to battle the bulge. Years of dampening and attempting to manipulate our natural hunger signals have left our bodies in a state of disarray. There's no doubt this has led some adults down a path of overzealous eating to the extent that when seated in front of a plate of food, they can't help but feel compelled to inhale it and lick their plate clean and then take seconds or thirds. Coupled with imitation foods that are suppose to 'trick' your body into feeling full like diet shakes and low calorie alternatives, these sick dieting methods aren't fooling anyone's belly. **You don't need to be underweight to be starving for real, healthy and satiating food.**

It's social norm, a sign of discipline and 'good' parenting, to enforce this rule of eating everything on your plate to our children. You can hardly blame parents though, as this was part of something they were taught by their parents and something their parents taught to them.

Stepping back a couple generations, during the Great Depression, cleaning your plate meant something entirely different. Food shortage was a real threat and this pressure was echoed throughout every corner of society. Compare this to the world we live in today. Whilst this threat is still imminent and a stark reality for many, for a vast majority of us, it remains a distant concern. Right now we have plenty and we do not suffer the dire consequences of starvation. We are part

86

of a generation that has never, and will probably never, experience such a harsh reality.

Simply viewing the solution as being a matter of eating what's on our plates rather than seeing it being scraped into the garbage is not an accurate reflection of the real challenges we face in our current state as citizens of the modern world. If we consider the amount of food we have the freedom to waste each year, it's clear that a lack of food is not the problem either. While we most certainly lack nutritional food in our diets if you're referring to the standard American/Australian/British (insert nation of choice) diet, eating all the food on such a dieter's plate would only exacerbate the obesity epidemic and move us further away from addressing the root of the problem.

Our problem is our attitude towards food.

To fix this problem, *we must fix our attitudes*. Consider this.

Imagine if you had to grow every tomato, harvest every apple and fetch every egg for the food you eat on your plate today. For every single meal, every single day, every single week, month and year. You get the point. This might even be a reality for some of you!

If we were each responsible for manufacturing our own candy bars, potato crisps, and frozen pizzas, many of these foods would quickly lose their appeal. They contain ingredients that are both highly complicated to obtain and involve resource intensive operations to process. That's right, *frozen pizzas don't just grow on trees*. Just like most things, man dipped his green thumb into the bucket of black paint and set about industrializing the food system, seeking greater manufacturing efficiencies for greater margins and profits.

Now consider this.

Most of us don't have the skills or time to learn how to service our cars. So we outsource this work to someone who can do this work for us in a far more efficient manner than we could ever dream of and we are more than happy to pay for their services to do so. So why are we so stingy with our dollar when it comes to paying for quality food produced in a sustainable manner? After all, this is the very energy that we are using to fuel our bodies; **to fuel our lives** so we can go forth and do other meaningful things as productive members of society. From this perspective, the precious energy and resources that go into creating these intricate and sustainable food systems are worth their weight in gold!

But we don't view it this way. When that same precious value is not placed on items in society where they should be placed, we are in essence, losing touch with our own personal values in life. Rather than fixing the problem, we attempt to mask it through every other means possible. It's like giving a child an aspirin for a minor cut rather than just dealing with it.

It's far too easy these days to view food as another mere consumable product. A commodity to be traded on the stock market that's treated under the same conditions as a lump of coal. When we don't have personal vested interests tied to our food production, it's easy to pass the accountability card to someone else. The whole process becomes some abstract notion. Doing this places you in a very disempowered position. Your job is not to merely shop and consume. Something about that just doesn't sit right. Such an attitude has landed us where we are now, where the average household throws out a third of the food they buy!

We need to understand as individuals and as a society that we are all accountable to the sustainability of our food system. You are part of the process as much as the grower. After all, the demand comes from the consumer. Producers will respond accordingly if there is more or less demand for a product. Food and water are the most precious resources on our planet and we often exert the least amount of energy tending to our personal needs for high quality standards and securing a safe future for our access to these things. Naturally, your shopping behavior will drive your eating habits so it's time to ensure these two align in your life.

Reducing our food waste should be priority. As individuals we need to take back some of this responsibility. While many of us aren't in direct control of our food production, you can take back ownership by supporting farmers who do promote a sustainable food system or by growing what you can and rethinking what and how you consume the rest. Food is precious and should be treated accordingly.

Here's what to do to reduce food waste in your household.

1. Serve your own food

At the table, it helps to allow each person to serve their own food. Whilst this may seem somewhat inhospitable, it gives each diner the freedom to determine how much they feel they can eat at that meal. Who's to say I didn't just down a steak before I came to your house because I was absolutely ravenous after work and surely enough, not feeling so hungry all of a sudden (bad guest manners, I know, but sometimes a girl's just gotta eat!). Allowing your guests to serve themselves avoids over-eating and wastage, helps the cook to estimate how much to prepare for next time, and leaves clean leftovers that can still be used the next day. After all, I can understand not wanting to eat someone's sloppy seconds.

2. You can always go back for seconds

Serve yourself less than what you would eat and only go back for seconds after you have finished your meal. Start to experiment with serving portions to find out what works for you. Until you get to the point where you can trust your body, you may wish to use your mental recollection to guide your eating choices. Think back to your level of activity that day, what else you've eaten and make an informed judgment on how much you think you would need to feel satisfied, not how much you want based on your plate size or some other emotional reasoning. Eat to nourish and fuel, not to fill an emotional void.

3. Teach your kids to eat intuitively

Feeding kids? Teach them to listen to their body's hunger cues. Guide them in their eating choices but ultimately, you want them to understand how to listen to their body and not being directed by external forces to eat or emotional cues. Helping them to develop a healthy relationship and teaching them about food wastage is critical for their personal development. Serve them enough to ensure they are being well-fed and nourished, but not so much that it forces them to eat beyond their natural inclination or where there is food wastage.

4. For the love of food, don't throw out leftovers!

Don't be scared of leftovers! They aren't out to eat you. Rather than tossing your leftovers into the trash can, pop them into a container and eat them as your lunch the next day or freeze for another night's dinner. How many times have you thrown out leftovers only to realize that you need to buy lunch the next day when you could have eaten those leftovers? An added plus, a lot of stews and curries taste better the following day after the flavors have settled.

5. Save your fresh produce before it goes off

Fruit and vegetables losing their freshness can be cooked and frozen, preserved or cultured. They can be thrown together to make a delicious soup or juice. I know how tempting that weekly special is or how cost effective it is to stock up when produce is in season, cheap and readily available. I for one am a self-confessed meat hoarder. Seriously, when they reduce meat because it's close to it's use-by date, I just have to stock up. So go ahead, make use of it, but do so wisely. My own freezer is constantly being cycled through bulk purchases of meat and veggies. Just be sure to make use of them at some point! If you can't see yourself being able to make use of it all before they spoil, then give it away to a neighbor or do a big cook up and invite some friends over for dinner. Cook a meal to pass onto a sick family member. I can think of numerous times I've laid in bed on a Sunday morning feeling sorry for myself wishing someone would come knocking on my door with a big bowl of home-made chicken soup! Think these things through before you resort to the trash can.

6. Make food preparation a priority

We've lost touch with traditional methods of food preparation because we've lost touch with our priorities in life. Why should an hour of scanning your Facebook news feed, watching Youtube videos and updating your Twitter status take priority over preparing a healthy and well thought out meal? Our health has taken a back-seat and I will tout it until the day I die, that sick individuals make up a sick society and a sick food system exacerbates this vicious circle. I enjoy my time in the kitchen partaking in food preparation and cooking because I've made it a priority in my life. Therefore, I make time for these things in my daily routine. Sure, that means less time in front of the TV, but watching TV isn't a priority for me. Not knowing who kissed who on 'The Bachelor' will not bring any more value to my life than having a delicious home made and nutritious bowl of grass fed beef and vegetable stir-fry. In doing so, I've learned to truly appreciate the food I cook and the mere thought of wasting something that I've poured my heart and energy into would seem like a crime against mankind.

7. Plan ahead

Planning ahead also helps reduces waste. Depending on how frequently you shop, write a list and have a rough meal plan in order for the days ahead so you can buy food accordingly. This will help keep your budget in good shape too. Cooking can be something you look forward to if you make it exciting. How does a slow cooked chicken cacciatore with a sweet potato mash sound? Maybe you'd prefer red wine beef and mushrooms with parsnip puree or a warm pumpkin and apple harvest salad? I have these and many other recipes on my own blog to get you started. Spend just an hour of your week sitting down to sift through Pinterest and recipe blogs to uncover some exciting new dishes to recreate.

8. Make use of your foods scraps

Compost your food scraps for the garden or toss them to your chickens (or to the dog if it does an equally good job like our Labrador with his gut of steel). Green waste shouldn't be banished to landfill. It should be returned to Mother Nature to recycle back into nutrients that can reused for future food. If you have space to compost but don't grow food, the compost can be used for trees and other plants. If you don't have space to compost, there are still other options for recycling your food scraps. I have a comprehensive guide on urban composting available as a free download which you can access here.

9. Donate unwanted shelf items to charity

There are often charity bins in shopping centers or collection agencies where you can donate canned and packaged goods. Naturally, it's best to minimize your consumption of these things from the start but if you have a few extra piling up in the back of your pantry, that's a great way to do away with them. There are also charitable organizations out there who collect leftover restaurant produce to feed to those in need. If you are a owner of a food business, please, reconsider if the food you are about to throw out can be salvaged or used for other purposes by those in need. Of course, if it's inedible, rotten or unsafe for human consumption (common sense here people), then you know it's okay to do away with. Even then you should be composting. The question is, *what can we do to avoid those wasteful situations?*

10. Express gratitude!

Saying a blessing or prayer before and after your meal is such a simple and effective way to remind ourselves that we are so very fortunate for the food we have. By living more mindfully, you will be aware of things you previously acted on in autopilot mode, such as scoffing down food mindlessly and throwing out the rest without a second thought. When you express this gratitude, you help to bring your mind back to the present moment so as to avoid reverting to your old ways.

CHAPTER 18

The Health Implications of Modern Food

"About eighty percent of the food on shelves of supermarkets today didn't exist 100 years ago."
- Larry McCleary, Author of 'Feed Your Brain, Lose Your Belly'

Food just ain't what it use to be. Tainted by the touch of man, modern and processed foods should stand alone as their own food group with a warning label on them, "Proceed with caution." Equating a humble potato to a slice of highly-refined white bread is ridiculous. Their similarities end at the word carbohydrate. Beyond that, the potato will win the showdown every time.

We aren't just talking fast foods either. Whether through a gradual process over centuries, such as agricultural hybridization, or more rapidly through genetic mutation, the fruits and vegetables we eat today have drifted further from their ancestral roots of yesteryear. What were once wild, are now bred, even if naturally so, to be bigger, hardier, sweeter and more uniform in size. This enables mass-scale efficiency as we witness in modern agriculture. Sadly, it comes at a price. An article in the New York Times articulated this point by explaining, *"Wild dandelions, once a springtime treat for Native Americans, have seven times more phyto-nutrients than spinach, which we consider a "superfood." A purple potato native to Peru has 28 times more cancer-fighting anthocyanins than common russet potatoes. One species of apple has a staggering 100 times more phyto-nutrients than the Golden Delicious variety displayed in our supermarkets."*[27] Wild varieties are proven to be more nutrient dense and we are breeding these nutrients out of our food.

A clear example can be seen in modern wheat which is far from its ancestral origins. Heirloom grains such as Einkorn possess a completely different nutrient profile to genetically manipulated modern strands (even if it's only through the process of hybridization). Modern wheat holds less than half the micro-nutrients as ancient varieties, with 19-28% lower concentrations of Zinc, Copper, Iron and Magnesium over the last 160 years.[28] Ancient grains were hand processed through a series of soaking, sprouting and fermenting to disable enzyme inhibitors and make nutrients more accessible so the end product is more easily digestible. Modern wheat is highly refined, with every component separated from the bran to the wheat germ, often bleached, and added with a concoction of other additives and laboratory created ingredients to make up the standard factory processed wheat breads.[29] Even the supposedly healthier 'whole wheat' is often refined white flour with the bran re-added after the processing. Modern wheat is being grown in nutrient depleted soils and artificially 'refortified' once everything else has been stripped clean to create the illusion there's something more of worth in them other than calories.

Whether you won the genetic roulette and thankfully don't suffer from Celiacs or other autoimmune diseases that see to you throwing daggers at any gluten contaminated product, you may still want to proceed with caution. Many people, even those who are not diagnosed Celiac, experience differing degrees of sensitivities to modern wheat and grains; more specifically, the gluten protein within wheat that causes a chain reaction of health problems. In such cases, gluten is infamous for causing a raucous in our digestives tracks when ingested. The body views these gluten proteins as a threat and launches a defensive attack. The downside, its attack is like a nuclear warhead; damaging the very intestinal lining in the process. This opens an escape route for the gluten proteins to pass through into the blood system and wreak havoc on the body, resulting in a situation of 'gut permeability'. This presents the body with a pickle as it's difficult to absorb nutrients in such a state. Those sensitive to this gluten warfare, experience symptoms such as skin rashes, stomach aches, headaches, bloating, abnormal bowel movements, brain fog and the list goes on.[30] Gluten has even been linked to Autism[31] and increases risk of heart disease.[32]

Not to single gluten out, I'll make a point to mention its other friends deviously hunched over in the corner. The modern invention of synthetic additives and preservatives are notorious for their health and allergenic implications, especially for hyperactive little children. We have an obsession with refined, standalone and highly processed sugars (another modern phenomena). Look out for ingredients on labels such as maltose, glucose, fructose, lactose, evaporated cane juice, malt syrup, sucrose, high fructose corn syrup, dextrose and agave. And yes, even organic will get thrown in front of these. **Just because it's organic, doesn't mean it's produced sustainability or that's it's good for you.** I've seen organic canola oil on a supermarket shelf, so don't be surprised that marketing tactics like this exist (while I'm sure it was organic, canola oil is certainly on the list of refined seed oils that you do not want to be consuming). Artificial sweeteners the body cannot metabolize come with many undercover aliases such as aspartame, saccharin and sucralose. They disguise under the zero calorie mask but possess dark powers to manipulate the underbelly.

My personal radical transformation has been enough proof to steer me clear from modern food technology wherever possible and keep me on my real food journey. Removing gluten, processed sugars, artificial sweeteners and preservatives, alongside other inflammatory foods from my diet, and focusing on eating nourishing whole foods that promote good gut health, has healed my perioral dermatitis and digestive stress. Not to mention the amazing by-products of learning how to enjoy the process of cooking nourishing foods, the art of traditional food preservation, and learning for myself how my body responds to the food I eat. **My life has grown richer on all levels.**

Weighing up whether the modern food we eat on a constant basis is worth the negative impacts on our health and the environment is something you need to decide for yourself. It's worth experimenting with a whole and natural food diet rather than taking everything written on a package for face value. Start by experimenting for 30 days to see how you feel. This is nothing committal for the long term and it's not to say you can't enjoy your favorite fast foods ever again. It will give you a chance to see what real food tastes like though and to understand just how your body reacts to the food you eat. I can guarantee it will have greater positive implications on your life than you could imagine. You'll get an idea of what foods you can start incorporating in later chapters.

CHAPTER 19

The Three Twisted Sisters of Agriculture

"I'm not interested in sustaining a planet on life support. My goal is to use agriculture to regenerate the planet."
- Harry Stoddart, Ex-Industrial Farmer turned Sustainable Farmer

You might go so far as to refer to them as the three witches of agriculture but there's no point vilifying the food. It's not the food's fault what man has done to bastardize their existence. Food is neither good or evil. **It's just food.** The problem is how ingrained (pun intended) these foods have become in our modern diets and the way they are abused in modern agriculture which is not only damaging to our health, but to Mother Nature as well. Over 75% of the world's population relies on the three sisters; wheat, corn and soy, (in addition to the less vilified rice crop) for daily sustenance, either directly or indirectly, such as through factory-farmed meat.

Man's manipulation of the three sisters is a twisted fairytale of which we've turned *our* role upside down as the evil fairy-godmother. The scale to which we produce these crops is astronomical. In the US alone, 84 million acres of corn, 73.8 million acres of soybeans and 55.7 million acres of wheat were harvested in 2011 according to figures from the EPA. The three industries combined generated over $116 billion from sales. These are numbers that make up the land area and economies of whole nations. **It's BIG business.** So you can begin to understand why governments have a vested interest in protecting such industries. What it's doing to the environment and to our health is not even a passing thought. If we want to talk natural destruction, we needn't look much further than what makes up the base of our government recommended food pyramids and how it's infiltrated our whole food system. You need only to follow the money.

The fact that we trade these crops like mere commodities to such a scale, has contrived a food system into one that has nothing to do with food any more. Rather than producing to feed the hungry and *nutritionally starved* people of the world, we have placed monetary gains first; producing in order to capitalize on the exploitation of the land, water and the workers. We'll go into more detail about each of the three sisters in next three chapters.

CHAPTER 20

The Perils of Peak Grain and The Wheat Witch

"In fact, wheat has been modified by humans to such a degree that modern strains are unable to survive in the wild without human support such as nitrate fertilization and pest control."
- William Davis, Author of 'Wheat Belly'

Peak oil isn't the only concern for the 21st century. The Food and Agriculture Organization of the United Nations states that, *"...climate trends since 1980 have reduced annual global maize harvest by an estimated 23 million tonnes and the wheat harvest by 33 million tonnes."*[33] About 30 percent of the major global cereal crops may have already reached their peak yields according to new research from the University of Nebraska-Lincoln.[34] While increased levels of carbon dioxide in the atmosphere is beneficial to the growth of some plants in specific geographical regions, the subsequent rising temperatures and increased frequency of droughts are of greater concern. This research goes on to conclude that despite increases in technologies in an attempt to sustain these high yields, *"the associated marginal costs, labor requirements, risks and environmental impacts may outweigh the benefits."* A study conducted by a team of scientists at the University of California-Davis also states that high levels of atmospheric CO_2 decreases the amount of protein in wheat. They explain, *"... protein available (from wheat) for human consumption may diminish by about 3% as atmospheric CO_2 reaches the levels anticipated during the next few decades."*[35]

Wheat currently provides 20% of dietary energy for the global population and it covers more of earth's surface than any other food crop. Researchers suggest yields must grow by 1.7% each year to meet future food demand.[36]

The threat of lower crop yields and higher price volatility is posing a dramatic dilemma for future food security and it will be the economically poorest countries in the world who will suffer the most. Their reliance on these staple food crops exposes them to greater vulnerability. While the research suggests that wealthier countries consume higher amounts of animal products,[37] these economies still rely heavily on wheat, corn and soybean agriculture for export trade. Not forgetting to mention the unsustainable conventional methods of factory farming that utilize grains for animal feed.

In your own life, you can protect yourself from the potential impact of peak grain by reducing your reliance on grain products and the factory farm system. As discussed in a previous chapter, the validity of conventional nutritional claims about wheat are flawed and its calorie to nutrient density ratio is minimal. Future food security should focus on more sustainable and local food sources with an emphasis on nutritional density. Depending on where you live, more nutrient dense carbohydrates that can replace your daily slice of bread may include a variety of potatoes, sweet potato, yam, pumpkin, wild rices, fruits and other vegetables.

CHAPTER 21

The Corn Chronicles

"Corn is already the most subsidized crop in America, raking in a total of $51 billion in federal handouts between 1995 and 2005 - twice as much as wheat subsidies and four times as much as soybeans. Ethanol itself is propped up by hefty subsidies, including a fifty-one-cent-per-gallon tax allowance for refiners."
- Jeff Goodell, Author & Contributing Editor to Rolling Stone Magazine

Corn is a big deal, especially for you Americans out there. Responsible for 40% of the world's corn production and with over a third of farm land dedicated to growing this monocrop, American corn means big business. But it's far removed from its humble Aztec origins. This conventional corn available to the mainstream is not of the ancient varieties from centuries prior. The wild varieties Mayans cultivated sparkled the brightest ruby reds, sapphire blues and warm oranges, much like a rainbow; gems of the ancient world. All we see in the produce section of supermarkets are the hybridized sweet yellow variety. The kind that's high in fructose and lacking in any nutrients of significance.

A report released by Ceres, a non-profit organization advocating for sustainable development, states that corn crops are not only the most water intensive and heavily irrigated, but also "the most fertilized of all major U.S. crops" and "*every year millions of tons of nitrogen and phosphate fertilizer leach into groundwater and runoff cornfields into waterways.*"[38] During times of radical droughts, a warming atmosphere, extreme and unreliable weather conditions, and over-stressed aquifers, one could conclude that corn is not winning awards for being the most sustainable crop to grow.

Traditional farming techniques involve rotating crops to disrupt the life cycle of insects and diseases[39] and to introduce depleted nutrients back into the soil. Corn, as is the case with *all* monocultures, are highly susceptible to disease and pest infestations because there's no natural defense systems in place once an outbreak has occurred. The lack of these techniques in conventional farming, and relying on a single "cash crop" as a source of income, places the farmer's livelihood in a precarious situation. Take for example the potato famine that caused over one million people to starve in Ireland and a mass population exodus during the mid-1800s. The disease, known as 'potato blight', wiped out whole potato fields and because over two-fifths of the Irish population were reliant on this cheap crop as sustenance, they could not survive.

This isn't just a message for food growers. As consumers, we should strive to eat a diversified diet, not only to give our body the greatest chance of nutrient exposure, but to minimize our dependence on one sole food source for our survival. It's a lesson in self-resilience.

Increasing pressure from governments for farmers to meet rising demand and achieve higher crop turnovers and increased yields, has come at the cost of the environment. Mitigating the risks of disease and pest infestations through conventional methods has spurred a reliance on chemical herbicides, insecticides and fungicides; the kind that are largely responsible for the degradation of over 70% of the world's topsoil.[40] This layer of fertile soil, known as humus, is what we we need in order to grow food. **No topsoil, no food.** Simple as that. When topsoil is diminishing at 10 to 40 times the rate to which it's being replenished, you can understand the urgency of this food crisis we are buried under. Without topsoil and a well established root system from perennial crops (as part of a biodiverse growing system) to absorb this water (something annually harvested and chemically sprayed monoculture crops do little to provide for), what does trickle through seeps past the plants that need it most. *The ones we're trying to grow for food to feed the world.*

Over 20 billion US taxpayer dollars were thrown at corn agriculture in 2012 through government subsidies. You can't blame farmers for wanting a piece of this pie but the funding has resulted in a large production surplus. A drive through the American countryside reveals how extensive corn obsession has become. The USDA estimates 40 percent of U.S. corn crop is processed into ethanol for use as engine fuel. This still leaves 60 percent for use in evil genius-worthy and creative ways. Of that, 37 percent goes into livestock feed and 11 percent is made into processed food ingredients like corn flour, high fructose corn syrup, corn starch and cooking oil.[41] Products have been invented to use this surplus without consideration for the negative health and environmental impacts.

The corn that has infiltrated our food system is one you wouldn't even recognize in its natural form but it is consumed in unfathomable amounts. Once harvested, corn is pulverized to a point of unrecognizable being and turned into the health debilitating high fructose corn syrup which you'll find gracing the ingredient list of far too many processed foods. If a corn cob is lucky to escape such a fate, it's generally fed to factory farmed livestock like pigs, chickens or cattle.

Agriculture in itself is responsible for using 70% of the world's fresh water.[42] Coupled with the devastating flow on effects from deforestation to make way for these plots, *we're clearly running out of planet.* This comes at a significant environmental cost as we lose the most precious forms of animal biodiversity, not to mention the plants and trees that help to absorb our excess carbon from the atmosphere. We have all heard about the devastation occurring in the Amazon rainforest. The Amazon is 5.7 million sq km, 75% of the Australian land area. Since 1970, 1/6 of the Amazon has been cleared, mainly for beef, and increasingly for ethanol. While the use of ethanol as a biofuel emits fewer CO_2 emissions than oil, the widespread use of it as a replacement cannot be justified. Intensive farming practices in corn cultivation ultimately negate any positive benefit extracted from utilizing ethanol as an alternative fuel source. It's clear that ethanol has limited capacity as a renewable resource and may even be worse for the environment. Clearing a rainforest to grow ethanol creates a carbon debt 17-420 times any benefit that using it to replace fossil fuels could extract.[43] Scientific American explains, "*These issues include indirect land-use change, the conflicts between land for fuels and land for food, water scarcity, loss of biodiversity and nitrogen pollution through the use of excess fertilizer.*"[44]

It's evident that clearing *more* land to grow unsustainable, low nutrient crops to fuel the biofuel and factory farming industries is not succeeding in feeding the world or reducing long term carbon emissions. We need to encourage and reward more sustainable utilization of the land we already wield under our agricultural control. As a consumer you can do so by making more conscious choices about buying sustainably grown food and not supporting companies that exploit nature's resources.

Then there's the final concern of genetically modified corn. While only a small percentage of the edible sweet corn is genetically modified, 90% of the field kind, used for these other mentioned purposes, such as livestock feed, corn-based sweeteners, starches and oils that adorn the ingredient labels of many processed foods, are almost certainly manufactured from genetically engineered corn.[45]

It's time to rethink our relationship with this middle sister of agriculture. While on the culinary front, there are still organic heirloom varieties of corn available for purchase, it's otherwise wise to reduce your consumption of this food in its processed form. Get smart about reading labels and the alarm bells should ring every time you see an ingredient like HFCS (high fructose corn syrup) or modified corn. If you buy corn in its real, whole form, make sure it's organic. Until sustainable farming practices are more widely adopted, ethanol remains an environmentally *unfriendly* form of biofuel. From where we stand today, the most effective method of reducing your carbon emissions remains; **to minimize your usage of fossil fuels through better lifestyle choices and habits.**

CHAPTER 22

Not So Succulent Soy

"Hundreds of epidemiological, clinical and laboratory studies link soy to malnutrition, digestive problems, thyroid dysfunction, cognitive decline, reproductive disorders, immune system breakdown, even heart disease and cancer. Most at risk are children given soy formula, vegetarians who eat soy as their main source of protein and adults self-medicating with soy foods and supplements."
- Kaayla Daniel, Author of 'The Whole Soy Story'

The life of soy is rather depressing. It's a love story gone awry. With over 94% of soy grown in the US coming from genetically modified seeds, it's veered far from it's traditional place as a beloved fermented side dish in Asian cuisine. Organic and non-GMO soy, when fermented such as in tempeh, natto, real miso and fermented soy sauces, most certainly can be part of a healthy diet in moderation. You had better be sure to understand how that soy has found a place on your plate though. We consume it at such alarming rates, you probably don't even know that you are.

Soy is leeching into every corner of our food system. From livestock feed to discrete ingredients in our food. Mary Vance writes in her book, *'The Dark Side of Soy'*:

"Soy is everywhere in our food supply, as the star in cereals and health-promoting foods and hidden in processed foods. Even if you read every label and avoid cardboard boxes, you are likely to find soy in your supplements and vitamins (look out for vitamin E derived from soy oil), in foods such as canned tuna, soups, sauces, breads, meats (injected under poultry skin), and chocolate, and in pet food

106

and body-care products."

The soy used in infant formulas, tofu, soy milk, soy bean oil, soy nuts and soy protein derivatives, are most certainly not the kind you want to be consuming and doing more harm to your health than good. Due to the high levels of goitrogens, soy can negatively influence the functionality of your thyroid. Soy is also high in phytic acid which binds to other vital nutrients, like calcium and zinc, hindering your body's ability to absorb them. This is why the process of fermentation is employed to mitigate this nutrient blocking effect. Research, specifically into the health implications of GM soy consumption, reveals the potential for it to act as an endocrine disruptor and increasing cancer risks.[46] I'll also speak more on the matter of GMO food in the proceeding chapters.

We're relying on a system to feed us food that's grown in poor quality soils where we need to synthetically replace the nutrients that we are deliberately draining from beneath our feet by the very same processes of earth degrading practices! It's a mouthful and *it's insanity*! We've sacrificed food quality for food quantity. What's the point of growing *more* when it results in crappier, nutrient deficient food that doesn't fulfill our *real* nutritional needs and strips our soil for future generations? We don't even need to use psychic powers to look into the future. **It's happening all around us today.**

We can't continue to grow mass scale monoculture crops reliant on industrial chemicals and fossil fuels. If you want food security for the future, you need to start making the choices now of what you want that future to look like for you. Start making changes by adjusting your diet to reflect one independent of earth degenerative farming practices.

CHAPTER 23

The Sweetly Deceptive Step Sister: Sugar

"Sugar is the new tobacco."
- Cynthia Kenyon, Molecular Biologist

You didn't think I was going to let sweet sugar slide on by. It's been the discussion point of many late night candy binges. Derived from either the sugar beet plant (in that case, it's probably GMO) or sugar cane, it's highly processed, refined and addictive. To understand just *how* addicted we are as a society, you probably needn't look further than your own pantry. The items an average family consumes on a weekly basis are laced with sugar, or sugar derivatives. From soda, sweets, cookies, candy, chocolate, ice-cream, bakery goods and the list goes on. Society has a sweet tooth and the cavities to prove it. Even items you think are pure; savory dips and spreads, deli meats, 'natural' fruit juices, granola, prepacked snacks and frozen dinners, are laden with sugar.

Sugar sets off a chain of chemical reactions in the brain that resembles the effects of cocaine abuse.[47] *Any wonder we're addicted?* Sugar is a simple carbohydrate the body does one of two things with. It either utilizes sugar for instant energy or it stores it as fat. Period. It offers no nutritional benefit when singled out. Attributed to being the lead cause in driving the obesity epidemic,[48] sugar is also linked to cancer by elevating insulin levels.[49] It's the main culprit behind tooth decay.[50] Sugar also raises cholesterol[51] and increases your risk of type II Diabetes.[52]

Sugar beets are the primary crop grown in the US for the purpose of sugar manufacturing and up to 60% of these crops are genetically modified.[53] I've mentioned the number of undercover agents sugar uses to hide in your food. The easiest method to avoid it is to forgo processed food altogether. Rediscover the lost art of home cooking and baking. If you want to enjoy eating your food, prioritize your time so you can enjoy the process of *making* it.

Sugar is also naturally found in fruits and vegetables but these foods possess a complete nutrient profile which assists your body's natural ability to process them. Fiber plays a critical role here as it helps to stunt the insulin spike that occurs when sugar is ingested. Enjoy nature's sweet bounty in its real, whole form and your body with thank you for it.

CHAPTER 24

A Biff To Pick With Beef

"We need to respect the fact that cows are herbivores, and that does not mean feeding them corn and chicken manure."
- Joel Salatin, Farmer, Speaker and Author

The typical stereotype of an Aussie barbecue just wouldn't be complete without a sizzling steak. Alongside countries like America, Brazil and Argentina, we have beef ingrained in our culture. So much so, that it employs thousands of workers and provides a huge source of export income from nations with less access to grazing land. Now I love a good steak as much as the next true blue Aussie, but I can't emphasize enough the anti-factory farming sentiment. It's through this process, of feeding cattle a diet that consists solely of corn, soy and grain products, all of which are foreign to their natural diet of grass, that has drenched the beef industry's reputation at large with a bucket of dirty slime. It's no surprise how carbon intensive this production process is. In previous chapters, we explored just how detrimental this reliance on the three sisters of agriculture is to the environment. A mere one kilogram of edible, boneless beef requires a staggering 30 kilograms of grain to compensate for feed to the cow.[54] While some are quick to point the finger and damn all meat eaters to an eternity of blazing fire, they fail to address the whole picture. There are two separate stories played out. The one that links man's agricultural exploits and the mass scale production of these monocrops to factory farming. Then the one that advocates a sustainable and earth regenerative practice of raising livestock in their natural environments. You know, *outside on pasture*.

The ethics of raising cattle on grain-based diets, more specifically, through the use of industrial feedlots, is confronting. It's an unnatural substitute of food for their selective herbivore diet. It's a known fact in the beef industry that poisoning and death can occur when introducing grains to the diet of a cow too quickly. It's just not natural. Like most herbivores, cows are restricted to a small selection of food which they rely on to survive. To cows, that is grass. To the Panda Bear, that is bamboo. For a Koala; eucalyptus leaves. You take that food source away from the herbivore and they either cannot survive or as is the case with cattle, are forced to eat food that's unnatural to their diet and suffer as a result.

Pigs and chickens have a more varied diet being omnivores and they prefer to forage. Omnivores find it easier to adapt to external pressures (such as changes in climate, natural disturbances to their food supply, famine, etc) that force a change in diet. Think of the raccoon, the dog or the cat and many rodents. These creatures are scavengers and thrive in various scenarios. Humans are another testament to this omnivore resilience. Why then are cattle able to survive on a grain-based diet? It's the same story played out among our species. Just because we can, *doesn't mean we should*. Nor that it's even beneficial for us to do so. Let's firstly look at why cattle are fed grains and what are the consequences of this system.

Cattle are supplemented, alongside their standard diet of hay, straw and grass, with grain, soy, corn and other ingredients to increase the energy density of their diet. It's a common practice to "finish" cattle on grain during their last days in industrial feedlots. Farmers often pass on their cows to feedlots to manage this process. It is a fattening agent which produces the fat marbling in meat cuts highly touted in the culinary world. Yes, some people insist this is the "preferred" way to eat beef and results in tastier cuts and gees, *I may just be insulting the culinary world of beef by thinking otherwise*, but they are ignoring the bigger picture and the consequences of this modern culinary fetish. Having come to this realization myself, I turn my nose up at restaurant menus boasting their 100 day 'grain-fed' steak the size of a human head with a hefty price tag attached to it.

Some years age, I worked in the export industry spending my days stamping shipment papers predominantly for the exportation of Australian beef to Asia. In between mouthfuls of coffee-slurping to keep me awake through this tedious task, my eyes would bulge at the numbers. Over 60% of Australia's beef is exported. Given we have the land and a small population to support this, it's the processing of export-grade beef which is troubling. In most cases, 'export grade' is code word for grain-finished as it's so highly prized by these cuisines (such as the Wagyu preference in Japan, one of our largest export markets). It's a taste with a high price tag and because of that, attracts interest from Australian farmers as the Asian middle-class continues to expand.

As interest in organic and sustainably-produced food grows, **the producers will respond**. This trend is creating a market shift within the domestic Australian beef industry. The Australian government in 2014 introduced a new grading for beef called the 'Pasture-Fed Certified Assurance System' (PCAS). It's welcomed news for farmers too who can capitalize on this growing demand as certification helps provide a marketing edge for mass appeal. Executive Director Geoff Teys of Teys Australia, a national meat processing company, explains, *"I think it's the organic push that we've seen. It's the health conscious public out there who are demanding a healthier option."*[55]

As more people move towards sustainable lifestyle choices, these shifting market trends are testament to the power of your choices.

Raising cattle on grain-based diets requires more energy inputs than what is gained as an output; a fundamental flaw in the whole process that makes it an unsustainable food system. There are external consequences to our environment commonly disregarded by people who consider the bag of feed as being the only input to the whole equation and the dollar return on the other end. When you factor in the previous noted ratio of kilograms of grain-feed required to beef-output (30:1), and the correlated environmental impacts of grain agriculture on our environment, including monoculture farming, water wastage and larger rates of genetically engineered seeds being used, and the huge environmental impacts of industrial feedlots (construction, electricity, machinery),[56] the equation is suddenly unbalanced. Why aren't these things factored into the price? Sadly, the industrial food system prefers not to disclose this information, nor take into account the real cost of its business practices. If people knew the whole story, they'd probably find that grain-finished steak hard to stomach.

Speaking of stomachs, grain-fed animals have as much as 80% *more* of the strain of E.coli in their guts than their grass-fed counterparts according to a study by Cornell University.[57] It's no wonder feedlot cattle require large doses of antibiotics. Animals forced to live in high density and unsanitary environments, such as seen in cattle and chicken feedlots, are more susceptible to disease outbreaks. These confined conditions are also extremely stressful for the animals and stress is detrimental to the immune systems. When stress hormones are released into the bloodstream, this can negatively impact the quality of the final beef product. It's a clear waste of resources, unnatural and completely destructive to the earth and the animal.

A grain-based diet is acidic to the digestive tract as opposed to the alkaline promoting benefits of a plant-based diet.[58] This carcinogenic diet adds physiological stress on the body making it susceptible to sickness. As a result, these animals are highly vaccinated with antibiotics and hormones which are also used as a steroid agent to promote faster growth and fattening to produce a higher turnover of beef. What happens to the toxins from these drugs? Similar to humans, they get stored in fat tissue. I'm certainly not salivating over the highly prized, fatty-marbled, grain-finished cuts.

I recently sat next to a New Zealand dairy farmer on a flight over to the USA. Every year he heads to Georgia for seasonal work and was speaking to me about their start-up days. At the time, they had no other choice but to purchase ex-feedlot cattle as these were all they could get their hands on. That in itself is a sad realization. They knew full well from their own experience in New Zealand that raising cattle on pasture provided the most nutritious and highest quality product for the consumer and this was the system they wanted to replicate. Conventional milk cannot even begin to compete on that standard and the price is a reflection of the quality in this case. The problem being, the cattle they purchased *had never been exposed to natural pasture.* They were born and bred in the factory feedlot system. **The farmers had to teach the cattle how to graze.** When an animal has become so domesticated it's lost its natural instinct to eat as nature intended, then you know we've drifted far from the land of sanity as a society.

Pasture-raised cattle are treated more ethically and live a happier and healthier life. Raising cattle in this manner also has the potential to radically transform landscapes if managed using rotational grazing techniques. The natural process of recycling nutrients into the soil when they excrete and "dump," injects the earth with high levels of nitrogen for the next generation of grass to grow. Nature has a funny way of knowing how to take care of itself. Many sustainable cattle farmers relate their job to being more about grass and soil farming than the actual animals. This system naturally eliminates the need for synthetic nitrogen fertilizers. Substantial amounts of excess nitrogen from fertilizers often leach into waterways causing significant imbalances in our aquatic ecosystems. Within a holistic system, it's a closed loop that eliminates waste and creates balance.

The ethical raising of livestock is part of an intricate and sustainable ecosystem that is being used to regenerate the earth and provide highly nutritious food as a by-product across the globe. Animals raised on pasture using these methods (and this isn't limited to cattle), have a critical role to play in regenerating natural habitats while simultaneously feeding people nutrient dense food. They prune the grass and stomp in their manure that all works together to produce a healthier ecosystem. The grass then does its job by sequestering carbon from the atmosphere, storing it in the root system and this all in turn builds healthy and nutrient rich topsoil. Cattle, sheep, bison, elk, kangaroos and other grazing animals, are able to convert energy (grass) that's directly useless to humans, into highly nutritional food. It's one of nature's most efficient systems.

We're seeing this story being played out across the world. If you haven't watched the TedX talk presented by Allan Savoury about intentional cattle grazing and rotation, I highly encourage you to do so. *Man has to manage the process though*. Not through industrial processes that only see to animals being cooped up in concrete floored feedlots and force fed on a fattening and health degrading grain diet.

A new standard needs to be set where farmers are encouraged and supported to farm as not just farmers, but land carers. Where they don't just have to 'get by' in order to make a living but where we give them an equal opportunity to make *just as good of a living* like those of us who are sitting at a desk banging on our keyboards all day. We can help these farmers by supporting them in buying their high-quality, sustainably-raised meat with our dollars. Contrary to common belief, the difference in the cost of grass-fed to grain-fed isn't that great. Especially when you factor in the *real* cost associated with raising livestock and the long term implications. Feedlot operations certainly do not factor the environmental degradation into the cost of their product. The positive environmental benefits of pasture raised cattle is light years ahead. Consider it an investment with high dividends for future generations.

Speaking directly to a farmer, you may also discover opportunities to buy in bulk, participate in herd share programs or receive cheaper cuts at a discounted price. I'm able to pick up around 2-3 kilograms of grass-fed, organic beef bones straight from a farmer at my local markets for around $6. I use these to make bone broth. This is mineral and collagen rich, gut healthy stuff! Nutrient density to dollar value is through the roof in my humble opinion.

Grass-fed beef is naturally leaner by nature because the cattle are required to 'work' for their good; grazing on pasture all day rather than being trough-fed grains in a feedlot stall. Even if you have a preference for the fattier cuts of meat as I do, (because yes, saturated fat is good for us contrary to conventional wisdom)[59], grass-fed beef has higher levels of CLA (Conjugated linoleic Acid) fats and 2-3 times more Omega 3 fatty acids than conventional beef.[60] These Omega 3s are formed in the chloroplasts of the green leaves and algae found in the pastures they are grazing on. The cows are turning an inedible plant into more readily, bio-available forms of these nutrients. Their four stomachs are doing all the hard work for us! Grass-fed meat is more nutritionally dense across the board. It has higher levels of antioxidants (vitamin E & beta-carotene), B-vitamins (in particular thiamin and riboflavin) and minerals (calcium, magnesium and potassium). A healthy cow raised on pasture eliminates the need for synthetic hormones and antibiotics.

As for the future of meat, if we don't act now, things could distastefully change. Scientists are already jumping on the opportunity to use stem cell research to grow meat in a petri dish.[61] Where's the earth regeneration in this picture? While the cost of this research will keep it off our supermarket shelves for some time yet, this kind of reality could very well be in our generation's future. Is that really what you want, *to be eating food from a petri dish?* Support the farmers who are creating a sustainable future for food. If you choose to eat meat, re-evaluate what constitutes an adequate and sustainable portion on your dinner plate. As with all food, eat in balance.

CHAPTER 25

Teenage Mutant Ninja Tomatoes: What's the Go with GMOs?

"We have entered an era of genetically modified foods, which are just that — genetically mutated foods that are not necessarily better for you. The health implications not only to humans but also to the environment is a hotly contested debate; the introduction of genetically altered food could have serious consequences, such as allergic reactions and increased resistance to certain antibiotics. Two of the prime targets for genetic engineering — soy and corn — are America's cash crops."
- Brenda Watson and Leonard Smith, Authors of 'The Detox Strategy'

Genetically modified organisms (GMOs) have been on the commercial radar for over 15 years. This laboratory process involves injecting an isolated gene from a foreign plant, virus, animal or bacteria, into the DNA of an unrelated plant or animal. They come with promises of higher yields and pest resistance and many farmers testify to their effectiveness. Except it's not that simple. There are downsides and the consequences are slowly peeling away from the hype. Evidence is accumulating to suggest longer term studies are needed before the government deems them safe for public consumption. Public consensus would agree. It does not eliminate the need for pesticides which is a fundamental concern about industrial agriculture for many people. There are grave consequences of this for natural ecosystems as I'll go into more detail soon.

The politics and passion behind the scenes has created heated debates between government, farmer and consumer. There's big money on the table. Companies have invested billions of dollars into research to develop these technologies. Farmers who have their whole livelihoods banking on these cash crops and are trapped in the cycle. Consumers who want transparent labelling so they can make well-informed decisions for their families. And governments who, well, *want to win the next election*. People either have their knees deep in gold, hold strong opinions or have a heck of a lot of self-interest to protect regardless of what side of the fence you stand.

GMOs aren't about to go away overnight. While some countries have proceeded with caution, others have bounded ahead in the uptake of this technology. Of all soybean crops planted in 2013 across the US, 93 percent involved GMO, herbicide-tolerant (HT) variants, the USDA acknowledged in a recent report.[62] In second and third place comes HT corn and HT cotton, making up about 85 and 82 percent of total acreage.

One of the greatest GMO controversies to hit our shelves can be rewound back to 1994. This was the year the 'Flavr Savr' Tomato hit the US market and became the pin-up boy for GMO food. Commercial tomatoes are normally picked prior to ripening and artificially ripened at a time closer to market. This bioengineered variety was bred with a deactivated gene to allow the tomato to fully ripen on the vine but maintain their shelf life for an extended period after that. Their fame was short-lived after a Hungarian-born biochemist, Dr Árpád Pusztai, subsequent to the release of his own research, vocalized on television that he would not personally consume genetically modified foods due to health concerns.[63] This caused a media stir and widespread boycotts of the product. The Flavr Savr tomato was officially retired in 1997 but left a sour taste in the mouths of consumers about the potential of GMOs to harm health.

The other major concern for GMO crops is their continued reliance on herbicides to curtail weeds. While there are some reports it has reduced the use of insecticides, it's increased the dependence on herbicides.[64] A rapid evolution of spray-resistant weeds is taking place. These 'super-bugs' and 'super-weeds' aren't worthy of comic book fame either. Think of them as pests on steroids; *sturdier and stronger than ever before and able to withstand higher amounts of chemical sprays than their predecessors.*[65] According to the International Survey of Herbicide Resistant Weeds, 438 unique cases of herbicide resistance have been reported to date.[66] **Our monoculture crops just got a whole lot greedier.** An unforeseen amount of money needs to be poured into continued research and technology to keep ahead of the game but in order to achieve this, these products need to sell to raise this kind of money. There's a far greater agenda served behind the scenes than growing food to feed the masses.

The particular culprit I want to bring to your attention here is the chemical 'glyphosate'; a herbicide marketed as Roundup manufactured by the largest GM seed company, Monsanto. Genetically engineered crop are 'Roundup-ready', meaning, they have been genetically modified to withstand the ill effects of glyphosate. It's the most widely used herbicide across the globe. From the groceries you buy at the supermarket, to the public parks your children play around in, to your neighbor's front yard and road side-walks. The spray drift and residue of this chemical, misleadingly deemed 'safe' by the industry as being both biodegradable and harmless to human health, is everywhere.

Monsanto, *commonly pitted as the evil villain*, was found to be guilty of false advertising by the French Courts in making these 'safe' claims and its Roundup product has been deemed an environmental hazard by the European Union. This has not stopped the corporate giant from encroaching its tentacles to other nations more vulnerable both economically and environmentally. In my recent travels through Central America, I saw billboard after billboard advertising this product. It's sad to see nations so rich in biodiversity, and even untouched by modern agriculture in some areas, facing a future of degradation and exploitation at the hands of Western greed.

The decline of the beautiful Monarch butterfly is linked to the use of glyphosate. *"Monarch butterfly populations are declining due to loss of habitat. To assure a future for monarchs, conservation and restoration of milkweeds needs to become a national priority,"* explains Chip Taylor, Director over at the non-profit 'Monarch Watch'. Migration numbers have plummeted in recent years, a huge tourism draw card for both the US and parts of Central America. The milkweed plant is the only habitat for the Monarch caterpillar and it's the very plant our use of glyphosate is targeting. This twisted perception that these plants serve no other purpose in an ecosystem other than to jeopardise the growth of our food crops is misguided. Spraying these plants also jeopardize the existence of our greatest pollinators, bees. Without bees pollinating many fruits and vegetables we rely on, our food system would fall flat.

These chemical sprays promote resistance in those very same weeds its purpose is to exterminate. This is evidence that we're fighting a losing battle. Evolution is nature's defense mechanisms kicking in. Mother Nature will continue to fight for survival so long as we butt heads with her. Extermination does not work. To what point is this sustainable if we continue to jeopardize the environment and our health?

This raises the question though, how do these chemical sprays, glyphosate in particular, affect your health directly? While we aren't suddenly going to keel over and die, the health implications are subtle and long term exposure to even low levels of these chemicals is detrimental to your health. Research links health effects on the neurological, respiratory, reproductive and dermal level along with increased cancer risk.[67] There are even greater risks involved for people who work with these chemical sprays on a daily basis. It's common practice in impoverished communities where both a lack of education and safety equipment causes improper handling of these toxic chemicals.

Concern lies in the long term damage these sprays are doing to our bodies on a cellular level through inflammation and in disturbing the balance of bacteria in our guts. The first generation of 'spray victims'

- this could be your friends, family or even self - already manifest many of these chronic diseases that are commonly associated with Western diets, such as obesity, diabetes, heart disease, autism, gastrointestinal disorders, infertility and even cancer. Each generation has the potential to genetically pass on health abnormalities.

The primary food groups of the Standard American Diet (SAD); that being, wheat, sugar, corn and soy; contain significantly more residual amounts of glyphosate because they are commonly grown using genetically engineered seeds (which you now know are manipulated to be resistant to this spray hence they're heavily sprayed with it). That's another strike on the ever growing list as to why you should reconsider consuming these foods as part of your diet. These residues *"enhance the damaging effects of other food-borne chemical residues and toxins in the environment to disrupt normal body functions and induce disease."*[68]

This extensive research into the effects of glyphosate on human health conducted by Anthony Samsel and Stephanie Seneff, asserts that *"Glyphosate's inhibition of cytochrome P450 (CYP) enzymes is an overlooked component of its toxicity to mammals. CYP enzymes play crucial roles in biology, one of which is to detoxify xenobiotics."*

What this means is that glyphosate targets the particular pathway of bacteria in your body, effecting how they metabolize essential amino acids (ones that can't be produced internally and must be extracted from what you eat). You are relying on the ability of your gut microbes to effectively process the food you eat in order for these nutrients to be bioavailable for your body to absorb. These little guys are the mice on the treadmill doing all the hard work in your body. So while glyphosate *may not directly* affect humans, it does affect us **indirectly** by damaging the pathways of our all important gut bacteria. This is vitally important because **our health is hinged on the health of our microbiome!** Without these bacteria and enzymes working effectively, we can't process the nutrients we eat (hence, the potential here for nutritional deficiencies) or expel other harmful environmental toxins. This leaves your body more vulnerable to the negative, compounding effects of multiplying pathogens.

Your body is a mass accumulation of bacteria that work together to help maintain a healthy and balanced environment. These good guys (the probiotics) need to be nurtured and protected. Consuming glyphosate causes an imbalance to this environment in your gut which allow pathogens to outnumber the beneficial microbes, otherwise known as the condition "gut dysbiosis." When the bad pathogens outnumber the good guys, your body becomes a breeding ground for a host of chronic health problems such as food allergies, gluten intolerance, leaky gut syndrome and inflammation. The effect of glyphosate on your health is serious, as it is a prime instigator in promoting an unfavorable environment for your beneficial gut bacteria which competes with the already increasing amounts of by-toxins (such as ammonia) being produced by the pathogens. **Glyphosate inhibits your body's natural ability to detoxify itself!**

There's a stark correlation here as to the rise in gut-related health illnesses and chronic lifestyle conditions with the advent of glyphosate-laced products available on the market in the 1970s. The research concludes glyphosate is a textbook example of how external toxins in our environment can negatively damage our health and disrupt our natural state of homeostasis.[69] That serving of glyphosate on your dinner plate doesn't look so appetizing after all.

Those pro-GMO argue it's the only way to feed the growing global population. That's a lot of pressure for anyone. Why would anyone want to throw all their eggs in one basket? Corn, soy, and other major GM crops are not the holy grail of nutrition and sustenance. For the sake of our health and longevity, we require an abundance of essential vitamins and minerals only obtainable through a diverse diet. We have an earth abundant in thousands of natural plant and animal species to fulfill these needs. More focus needs to be invested in fostering the next generation of land carers who can grow these foods in smaller-scale, sustainable, polyculture systems. Let's not forget the governmental, fiscal and economic reform that's required in order to break down the barriers stopping those in need from gaining food independence. We all have a part to play in feeding ourselves, and supporting a sustainable food system to feed those around us.

There is enough evidence to suggest that we are in the throes of a mass-scale science experiment that does not support alternative solutions for protecting or regenerating the earth's resources. I for one, do not choose to be a guinea pig. You can help by taking responsibility for at least some of the food you consume, if not all, through growing our own or knowing who is.

Here's a list of common GM foods or GM containing products:

- Any processed food that contains high fructose corn syrup

- Vegetable and seed oils such as Canola Oil, Soybean Oil, and Cottonseed Oil (these are common ingredients used in mayonnaise, cakes, cookies, snacks, muesli bars and chocolates)

- Breakfast Cereals

- Products that contain sugar derived from sugar beets (common in frozen foods and is the primary form of sugar used in the US)

- Artificially sweetened juices

- Carbonated soft drinks and sodas

- Baby Formulas (often contain GM soy and corn)

- Factory farmed meat (animals are fed a soy and corn rich diet)

- Dairy products (again, from factory farmed animals)

- Eggs from chickens fed a diet of soy and corn

- Hawaiian Papaya

- Tofu, soy milk and other soy derived foods used as meat substitutes

- Chocolate (with soy lecithin and emulsifiers)

- Modified corn starch (used in cakes, cookies, snack bars and cereals)

CHAPTER 26

The Great Debate: Conventional vs Organic Food

"Agricultural sustainability doesn't depend on agritechnology. To believe it does is to put the emphasis on the wrong bit of 'agriculture.' What sustainability depends on isn't agri- so much as culture."
- Raj Patel, Environmental Journalist

Organic and conventionally grown foods are pitted against each other like it were a worldwide wrestling match. Sponsored journalism and selective studies have left a carefully marked trail of evidence proclaiming there is no difference in nutritional quality when compared side-by-side. Dig deeper and you find some of these studies sponsored by non-independent bodies, such as the agrochem companies themselves.[70] The credibility of these studies is questionable and the argument ignores a huge piece of the jigsaw puzzle, leaving the public confused and in a state of health and mental disarray.

It's not just about the nutrition. Failure to understand the macro effects of these conventional pesticides on the environment and consequently, how they affect our health on the micro level, leaves the argument comparing only nutrition. The definition and practices behind organic farming vary greatly. There are reports from drought-stricken California where large scale organic carrot and wheat fields are exploiting groundwater to the point the aquifer is being depleted twice as fast as it's being replenished.[71]

Slapping an organic label on something does not make it more nutritious or environmentally sound nor can one conclude from a few studies that it is the same as conventionally farmed food because there are too many variables. It's not a case of apples and oranges but nor is it even a case of apples and apples. Micronutrient deficiencies are becoming a huge problem in both the developing and industrialized worlds.[72] This trend over the last several decades has coincided with the diffusion of industrial agriculture as the focus has shifted further away from producing high quality, nutrient-dense food and replenishing soil integrity. Conventional farming relies on high cost capital facilities and technology, large inputs of synthetic fertilizers and pesticides and in a manner that depletes soil quality to extract high yields. Low nutrient cereal grains dominate the market which later need to be further processed and 'fortified' with vitamins to replace these lost nutrients.[73] Food will only be as nutritious as the soil it is grown from and greater emphasis needs to be placed on feeding people the nutrient dense food we need.

The organic farmers I have spoken to, visited and worked with, practice natural pest management strategies like multi-crop rotation to break pest cycles, promote biodiversity, practice close-knit planting and heavily focus on well balanced soil health to deter weeds. Their processes do not involve relying on synthetic fertilizers or pesticides to produce a crop yield. Knowledgeable and responsible farmers seek ways to restore soil health first and foremost.

There is no global standard for what constitutes organic certification and nor would this be practical. Check with your state or national regulatory body to understand what exactly it means to have an item wearing such a label. Some processed items are allowed to carry the certification even if only containing a percentage of organic ingredients or food grown from farms that utilize a number of approved organic sprays. *Confusing, right*? For example, in the US, there are three levels of certification; 100% and 95% can bear the USDA certified organic seal while on the other hand, 70% organic cannot (but the company may list the ingredients on the packaging to state which are organic). Wikipedia has a great reference for individual country labeling laws around Organic Certification. Keep in mind attaining certification is a costly exercise for some small producers and they purposefully choose not to for this reason. Speak with them directly about their farming practices to understand their circumstances.

Buying organic, but more importantly, *sustainably*, means so much more than nutrition. Many conscious consumers buy organic to avoid toxic chemical residue on their food, to avoid GMOs, as preferred taste, on an ethical basis or because of their relationship with the farmer and the cultivation process. Sustainable farming factors in the long-term costs of agriculture and this is reflected in their price. There are significant downsides to conventional agriculture which do not factor in the external costs of their production; the use of harmful chemicals, imbalances to the native ecosystems, soil degradation and livestock welfare. These are overlooked in their price and give the consumer a false sense of the real cost of food.

At this point in time, I understand not everyone can afford the higher price tag of what some organic food can cost and I'm not about to jump down your throat and declare you to prioritize your finances in order to so. That's your decision but I encourage you to look for creative ways to make it more feasible.

Until it becomes the norm, here are a few tips you can take on board to help cut the costs of buying organic.

- Buy what's in season and can be produced locally. This will mean adjusting your diet to fit the seasons. Tropical fruit in winter will always cost more as it's most likely being shipped in from miles away. In winter, our bodies crave warm, earthy foods like root vegetables. It makes intuitive sense.

- Support a local Community Supported Agriculture (CSA) program. This is where you pay an upfront cost to the farmer who will then provide you with a box of farm fresh food each week throughout the growing season. These programs can cut the cost of buying organic food because it's farmer-to-consumer direct, cutting out the middleman.

- Sometimes towards the end of closing, seller's may discount their food at the Farmers' Market just to get rid of it. You may be limited to choice though.

- Stock up on weekly specials and cater your meal planning around those. Any excess produce can be cooked up as meals to freeze for future use.

- Grow vegetables that are more expensive to buy or that you use more of. Herbs are easy to keep in container pots and are the most cost effective plants you can buy. Most people buy a packet of fresh herbs as a once off garnish, to only need more after they've thrown a bunch out. If you have too many herbs, they are easy to chop up and freeze in a container.

- Buy organic, pasture-raised meat or that has been discounted because it's nearly past its shelf life date. You can then just cook it up that night or freeze it.

- Ask around if any farmer's offer herd-share programs for sourcing organic (and even raw) milk. This is where you collectively buy a 'share' in a cow which compensates the farmer for his/her time and energy caring for the animals and in return, you'll receive a share of the milk each week. It's like receiving a dividend from stocks!

- Buy in bulk. There are cooperative stores that have bulk bins you can buy organic nuts, seeds, honey, flours and other foods for at a cheaper price than the equivalent single product on the shelf.

- Go online and see if there's a 'Buying Club' you can become a member of. These clubs take periodical orders from members so they can purchase large quantities at wholesale price and disperse between the club members.

- Buying a whole animal and having a butcher divide up the

meat is far more economical in the long term. Naturally, this only makes sense if you have the freezer space but you may have enough meat to last a whole year! The alternative could be to split the cost and divide up the meat with friends or family.

- There's the famous 'Dirty Dozen' of vegetables and fruits that are most commonly, heavily sprayed. So if you can only afford to spend a portion of your weekly budget on organic food, these should be priority; apples, strawberries, grapes, celery, white potatoes, spinach, bell peppers, tomatoes, cucumbers, nectarines, blueberries and snap peas.

- Many people find that after reducing the amount of processed foods in their diet, this frees up extra money to spend on higher quality, more nutrient-dense fresh foods.

CHAPTER 27

The Economics of Your Food Choices

"Don't dig your grave with your own knife and fork."
- English Proverb

Do you eat for yourself or do you eat or the world?

It's a loaded question but just think about it for a moment.

Of course we eat for ourselves. We eat to live. Our bodies require the nutrition and the calories or else, we may as well be standing in line at the post office and perishing away a slow and painful death.

We give little credit to the impact that these personal choices have on the greater good and how this affects our own quality of life. The system you support will be the system that supports you. We can't perpetually fight an existing system of big corporations, fast food giants and GMOs that aren't about to step down or even budge any time soon. If we pour all of our energy into *fighting*, it leaves no room for *restoring and* building the kind of food system we can influence more directly and immediately. So save some energy for that.

If you expect organic vegetables, pasture-raised meats, high quality this and that, you can't just talk about it. You actively need to be involved in the process and the economic circle of exchange. There's the supply and demand model that comes into play which I can thank my 'Economic Principles' professor for teaching me. *I have to put that business and finance degree to some use.*

So what are the economics of your food choices?

Micro Food Choices

Consider the food choices you make that affect you directly. We all are striving for optimal health and longevity so there's no discrediting the importance of these micro food choices. After all, this dictates your actions on the macro level and they interplay with each other. On the micro level, this is the food you choose to eat based on its health and nutritional benefits to you (or lack thereof in some cases). You question whether this food promotes or *demotes* health. Eat from a stable place of self care and love; not through fear or guilt of 'bad' foods.

Contrary to mainstream fad diets, a real food diet varies from person to person based on seasonal and geographical reasons. Working within the sustainable guidelines and depending on your nutritional needs and dietary restrictions, it makes sense to eat a diversity of natural foods including; grass-fed, organic and pasture-raised meats (including utilizing bones and organ meats), wild caught fish, organic and sustainably grown fruits and vegetables, unprocessed dairy (like raw milk and cheeses), nuts and seeds, an abundance of fermented foods and of course, a hefty dose of healthy fats like coconut oil, olive oil, old fashioned lard, tallow, butter and ghee. Strive to minimize your consumption of processed and prepackaged foods. A good way to address this is by keeping things simple. Avoid companies that spend ridiculous amounts of money on advertising. Buy local and direct wherever possible. Minimize the parties involved in growing and processing your food. Turn to nature, not the laboratory, to fulfill your nutritional needs.

Macro Food Choices

This looks at the greater impact of your food choices. Do you buy your food from a sustainable local farmer who grows food organically using regenerative farming practices? Are you paying a fair price for this food? Do you consider the number of food miles it's taken to bring that food from the farm to your plate? Is it imported - coming with the bonus side of a heavy carbon footprint? Has it been produced through the exploitation of cheap offshore labor under conditions that leave no room for environmental conservation? Do you buy your food from the corporate mega-mart, fast food conglomerates or from the small guy at the farmers' market? Understand the why and hows of where it's been sourced from. What environmental impact do such food habits have in both the short and long term?

The acronym '**SLOW**' can be referenced as a guide to sustainable eating.

Seasonal

Shop and eat food when it's in season based around your local environment. This is the way we were born to eat and your body even craves certain foods based on seasonal availability. Winter just screams for warm, earthy root vegetables whilst summer is all about fresh, crisp and light tropical fruits. Foods in season make sense financially too as they are more affordable because of their abundance. Anything that's not in season in your little corner of the globe has to be imported from elsewhere and this is a drag on the environment due to transportation costs and fuel which ultimately, comes out of your wallet. So even more reason to celebrate the coming of each new season with the excitement of new foods!

Local

By supporting local farmers and buying locally, or taking it one step further and growing your own food, you are helping to secure the future of food production in your area for future generations. It'll taste better too. Apples imported from overseas can be frozen for up to 12 months. *No thanks.*

Organic

Beyond organic, one should also consider the sustainable nature of how their food is grown. The basic premise though, is to minimize your exposure to potentially harmful chemicals and toxins, increase your uptake of quality nutrients and support farmers who are doing the right thing by the land. More information about this topic is covered in the previous chapter.

Whole

Eating a variety of foods in their real, whole state is optimal for sustenance. Vitamins and nutrients interact with each other when foods are consumed in their whole form, assisting your body to process them more readily. Opt for the whole apple rather than apple juice. The fiber assists your body to feel fuller for longer. 'Food' manufactured in laboratories are not fit for human consumption. Chemicals and additives that are pumped into processed foods take away from your health rather than adding to it. Do your body a favor and get real. Empower yourself with knowledge (and help others in the process too) so you can make better choices to help promote the kind of world we all want to live in.

As I ripen (and sweeten) in age, I have learned that health is as much a lifestyle choice as it is a blessing. Yes, there are those born into ill health but for many of us, it's the lifestyle diseases such as diabetes and heart disease that are of greater threat to our existence. The prevalence of these 'lifestyle diseases' in modern society is a reflection of our sick food system, a serious lack and dispersion of education, truck loads of misinformation and an imbalance of priorities in our personal lifestyles. Drive the sustainable demand up and the supply will follow.

CHAPTER 28

Fashion Faux Pas: Green is the New Black

"Fashion is not something that exists in dresses only. Fashion is in the sky, in the streets, fashion has to do with ideas, the way we live, what is happening."
- Coco Chanel, Fashion Icon

I love getting dolled up as much as the next girl. So what thread do I have to pull with fashion? Fashion has been with us since the dawn of man. The moment Adam and Eve sported the latest in real "eco-fashion", *we were in for a wild ride*. While it didn't take us long to go from leaves to leather, we now see the revolving door of trends turning faster than ever. Whilst a perfectly acceptable form of creative expression for many, it has also become one of the most wasteful, energy intensive, exploited and shallow status symbols of our time.

The average American throws away over 68 pounds of textiles per year. That's synthetic, petroleum-based fibers that take decades to decompose going straight into landfill. While the clothing you wear is often produced from 'natural' fibers, you wouldn't dare touch them in their raw form with the amount of pesticides, insecticides, formaldehyde, flame-retardants and other known carcinogens that reside on their surface. If you think by just eating healthy and organic food you are eliminating your exposure to these chemicals, *think again*. We need to pursue a more holistic attitude towards fashion and across all areas of life if we're to live authentically sustainable.

From something as simple as being a means to keep us warm or for the most part (for the sake of social decency) *covered*, it has still played a significant role in human history if we care to admit or not.

At the end of the day, we all wear clothes. It's unavoidable.

On more than one occasion than I'd care to admit, I have bought new clothes to only have them disappear in the depths of Narnia at the back of my wardrobe and never see daylight ever again. Clothes are just one of a myriad of consumable products in our lives that we have little to do with the production process. The more disconnected we are, the easier it is for us to mindlessly consume with little thought beyond our color preference and what accessories will match. We've talked about consumerism at large in earlier chapters and by now, I hope you're beginning to realize that it is man's attitude towards these things that have dislodged our sense of accountability and responsibility to Mother Nature. This idea that the industry at large feeds off our insecurities may be true, but what can be said for the moving trends of every other consumerist product in our capitalistic world? We can't single out fashion on this premise.

Fashion isn't inherently shallow but it's the way it's portrayed, and sadly, *sometimes* the people it attracts, that often are. I do believe you can still have a healthy, balanced relationship with fashion like all else in our lives. It just depends how you go about it and the underlying motives. There is much to be said for the people who dedicate their lives to a creative process to only be left with a complete social misunderstanding towards their chosen art form. Even within these groups, I'd love to see a bigger push towards truly sustainable fashion, where the focus is on using organic, high quality clothing fabrics, employing fair-trade work conditions, and encouraging a more positive and meaningful producer and consumer experience.

Fast fashion (cheap and poorly made) is like fast food (cheap and with little nutritional value). It's not healthy for us nor Mother Nature; doing more long term damage than short term good. It's one that's driven by a high turnover of low quality goods at a low margin. Is it no wonder the mannequins wear a new outfit every other day? These conditions only perpetuate the mentality that fashion is fleeting and positions the consumer in constant state of dissatisfaction.

How can we change an industry that's driven by high turnover, small margins and that serves fast-paced, fleeting trends? **By changing the way we shop as consumers.**

If people knew that their fast fashion addictions supported astronomical water wastage, pollution of water, pollution of their own community, life threatening working conditions, exploitation of child labor, deforestation, GMO cotton monoculture and the list goes on, they would probably reconsider their purchasing habits. We, as consumers, deserve to be conscious of this knowledge so we can make more informed purchases. Here are some other helpful guidelines you can implement to help you enjoy fashion for what it is:

1. Stick to the seasons

Just like we ought to eat with the seasons, as should the seasons dictate our fashion choices. We have the privilege of disposable incomes that allow us to spend money based on *want* rather than *need*. This makes way for some pretty impulsive shopping habits. Does it really seem necessary to have a revolving door of fashion change on a weekly basis on top of the changing trends of the season? You can still enjoy playing with your fashion style but stick to the seasons. There's four seasons in a year, **not fifty-two**.

2. Wash less often, in cold water and line dry

When I say wash less often, I'm not talking about forgoing your personal hygiene. Unless you are sweating it out in the sun doing manual labor, chances are, your jeans probably don't need to be washed every single time you wear them. The sniff test goes a long way. In fact, constant washing is a sure way to faster deterioration. To extend the life of your clothes, wash less, in cold water and line dry. It also makes sense for your energy consumption. Tumble driers are some of the most energy hungry machines in your household. Make sure you also wash with a full load unless you have a machine that only fills with enough water based on the load weight.

3. Consume knowledge and ask questions

Don't be afraid to question fashion stores or brands about their supply chain. Do your research and if you don't feel confident or comfortable in supporting a brand because of the choices they've made and how they operate, then don't spend your money with them.

4. Don't buy it if you won't wear it

The weightless mannequin gazes pretentiously into the distance as it shows off the new season's 'must-have' hip-hugging number. It's been plastered in all the magazine editorials and the deep urge to have it is driving you crazy. Except you already have a similar outfit from last year hanging in your wardrobe, with tags still attached. But this one, it's 'different'. The deep urge of desire is driving you crazy. Caving in will make the feeling go away. Yes, that's the easy way out. Even though there's a part of you that knows you probably won't wear it, and the looming credit card bill will haunt you for nights to come. But, but, but....

In these situations of vulnerability, the credit card can spontaneously and magically find it's way into the cashier's hands. **STOP**. Before you even reach for the article of clothing, ask yourself if you really need it three times. Your first rationale is often related to 'wanting'. Being able to distinguish between 'want' and 'need' will help you recognize those times you attempt to justify the expense through sheer *want*. If this doesn't work, put it back on the rack anyway and walk away telling yourself that you'll just think about it and are free to come back the next week to purchase if you really do need it. The effort and time needed to go back to the store and mulling over it for a week (and realizing *you won't die without it*) will work in your favor to not go back.

5. Second-hand clothing

If you're on the hunt for a new outfit, start by sifting through the racks at second-hand and charity stores. You'll be able to use your own creative prowess to explore and create a unique fashion style. It not only saves you money, you can find great pleasure in piecing together your own outfits without someone else dictating what is hot and what is not. You can also host clothes swaps with friends or ask to borrow an outfit for a special event.

6. Mend and repair

From here, you may even start to dabble in the art of design, sewing and stitching. Who knows, you could have yourself a new hobby! Don't be so quick to toss out those pants or socks if a hole starts to show. It's time to brush up on those mending skills. There's still life in those clothes yet.

7. Stop window shopping

Remove the temptation to shop by limiting your exposure to clothing stores (both online and offline). This includes mindless online browsing and social media. Unsubscribe from retail email newsletters (the website unroll.me will provide a list of everything you are subscribed to). Most fashion purchases are impulsive. The less frequently you're exposed to the passing trends, the fewer chances you have of being influenced by the flavor of the week as dictated by so and so sitting behind their desk. Be your own fashion police.

8. Support ethically and sustainably produced brands

There are many fashionistas out there striving to make better choices for their wardrobe. Organic cotton, fair trade, sustainably produced and naturally dyed are just some examples of keywords to look for when investigating a label.

PART 5

PRINCIPLE 3
TO PROMOTE HEALTH AND WELLNESS

CHAPTER 29

Filling the Holes in Holistic Wholeness

". . . how and what we eat determines to a great extent the use we make of the world– and what is to become of it. To eat with a fuller consciousness of all that is at stake might sound like a burden, but in practice few things in life afford quite as much satisfaction."
- Michael Pollan, Author of 'The Omnivore's Dilemma'

When you hear the words "health and wellness," what are the first thoughts? Is it food, exercise, meditation or your faith?

All of these things are important and have a part to play in building a sustainable lifestyle. There is no one or the other. In the same way we can't ignore our responsibility to this planet, we can't forgo our responsibility to our own health and wellness. If you do so, you only inhibit yourself from effectively fulfilling the positive impact you can have on this world. A strong body, a strong soul, and a strong mind; these things all interplay with each other. In order to live out a sustainable life, you must first learn to care for yourself in a holistic matter, in all sense of the word. So first of all, let's explore what *sustainable eating* looks like and how this impacts your health and wellness.

1. Less packaging and more cooking

It's time to learn how to cook. When you cook at home, you have control over the ingredients that go into your meal. The more you get in the kitchen and practice, the more joy you'll extract from the creative process of combining and discovering new flavors. The earth is rich in its biodiversity and by exploring it more, you reduce your dependence on unhealthy, processed and packaged foods that come to you by way of a machine. You'll discover that you are indeed master over your own taste buds and you don't need to be reliant on another person dictating what you can and can't eat. Your Grandma really was onto something when she said her food is made with love!

2. Forgo the GMOs

By now you've most certainly become accustomed to the not so glowing reputation of these "frankenfoods." We explored the issue in great depth in the previous chapters.

3. Eat more fresh and locally grown produce

The closer you can buy your fresh produce from the food source, the better. This reduces transport miles, supports local farmers and results in healthier, tastier and fresher food for you. It's about ensuring a strong local economy where yes, people closest to you, have the opportunity to make a stable living that works in return to support you! It's about pouring money back into the community and "recycling" resources between those who can use them respectively. This works to strengthen the local economy so it's not affected as greatly to external pressures and crises.

4. Buy organic and sustainable

We explored the importance of organic and sustainably produced food in chapter 26. Don't be afraid to ask questions to learn more about best practices.

5. Grow your own food

What better way to take back control over our food system than to start growing your own food. This way, you can guarantee the quality and eliminate the need for synthetic and harmful chemicals. One of my favorite quotes is from LA based guerilla gardener, Ron Finley, *"Gardening is the most therapeutic and defiant act you can do. Plus you get strawberries."*

6. Ethically raised, pasture-raised meat

Just like any food you consume, it's important to know where it is coming from and what's gone into the production of said food. Meat is no exception. With steak being a personal favorite treat of mine, it's crucial to understand the nature of factory farming that has skewed our outlook on what constitutes ethically and sustainably-raised meat products. If you choose to eat meat, do so with regard to the traditional process that helps to sustain healthy animals and a healthy environment.

7. Don't throw the bones out

Again, if you so choose to eat meat, are you utilizing the whole animal or merely a select few popular and expensive cuts? The average consumer's preference and demand for lean, boneless cuts places significant pressure on the food system. Guess what? *Chicken don't come boneless in nature.* This leaves a huge black hole of waste for the less favorable parts of animals, that is, the organs, bones and tougher cuts. The often forgotten about bones and organ meats are the health industries biggest (but not so secret) nutrient gold mine. Not only are they some of the most nutrient dense foods you can eat, they are unpopular cuts of meat that frequently go to waste. Pop some bones into the slow cooker and leave to stew for 24 hours. The end result is a delicious and nutrient rich bone broth. I have an easy to follow recipe on my blog you can refer to.

8. Don't turn up your nose to the rejects

Supermarkets have standards they must adhere to sell produce. Fruits and vegetables need to be of a certain size, a certain color and without blemish. We've forgotten what real, organic and wild food looks like! Nature is not perfect and nor should the food on our plate look pristine and proper. Don't be afraid to venture into the unknown of the local farmer's market and pick out the imperfect rejects. No one likes to judge a book by its cover, right? You can even save a few dollars in the process as producers often sell these as discounted seconds.

CHAPTER 30

Natural Beauty From The Inside Out

"Sometimes people are beautiful.
Not in looks.
Not in what they say.
Just in what they are."
- Markus Zusak, Author of 'I am the Messenger'

When half the real estate within a magazine is filled with glossy pictures of photo-shopped celebrities and models brandishing beauty products, you can begin to understand that this is an industry feeding off some of our deepest insecurities.

The beauty industry is raking in over $400 billion a year and these numbers are only increasing as a burgeoning middle class obsessed with beauty is expanding globally.[74] This is not just a Western phenomenon. Beauty cosmetics is a *global* language both women and men understand.

It's so tempting to believe in these false hopes and promises these magazine advertisements present. They make you believe if you use what the professionals use, you can look like them too. By this logic, we would all be walking Paris Hilton clones. *No thank you.*

The decision to detox my beauty regime was one of the best decisions I made, not only for my body's health but also for my emotional and mental health. From the day I swore an oath to ditch the synthetic chemicals that my commercial moisturizers, cleansers, makeup and hair products were laden with; it was as though my body was finally allowed to let it all out *and just breathe*.

Many moons ago, my skin was at a crisis point. It was a gradual shift downhill that I should have seen coming. *The bubble was always going to burst.* It was just a matter of when. Hormonal disruptions from toxins in the environment around me, lifestyle stress, nutritional deficiencies; they were all contributing factors alongside the decline in my gut health due to several courses of antibiotics over the previous years.

As the little bumps and spots continued to pop up on my face, I felt like I had no other choice but to use more commercial products to cover them up. In panic mode, I invested in *more* cleansers, *more* serums, *more* pimple-busting exfoliants in hope of scrubbing the horrid things away. All in the hope of *washing away* the problem. Much to my horror, **they didn't help.** These very products were actually exacerbating the problem and wasting my time, energy and money.

I was trapped in a sick cycle of volcanic eruptions and connect-the-dot puzzles on my face. Whether it's acne, hormonal eruptions, dull and lifeless skin, or a multitude of other frustrating skin conditions, no one wants to be hiding behind a caked mask of make-up and it's no wonder people are praying (and paying) for a miracle. The average woman exposes her body to over 515 different synthetic chemicals through her daily beauty regime.[75] This may consist of a daily routine of face cleansing, toning, moisturizing, applying copious amounts of make-up, only to repeat this same process in reverse that evening and each and every day subsequent to that. *Carefully maintaining that mask.* Toppled with shampoos and conditioners, body washes, deodorants, styling products and perfumes, we are walking, fumigated, nuclear bombs of beauty products.

When you lather these chemicals onto your skin, a large percentage are absorbed directly into your bloodstream. Yes, *directly.* Do not pass go. **Do not collect $200**. Dr Barbara Olioso, an independent professional chemist says, *"Research shows that between 20 and 60 per cent of parabens may be absorbed into the body."* Parabens are preservatives used in most skin care products, soaps and shampoos and it interacts with our body in a very startling manner. In it's process of stopping bacterial growth (being the preservative that it is), it mimics the effects of the female hormone, estrogen, in our bodies which an excess of is known to promote cancerous tumor growth.

Aluminum, the salts of which are used as an active antiperspirant agent in common underarm body deodorants, has also been linked to breast cancer. Studies show aluminum is known to have a genotoxic profile, capable of causing both DNA alterations and epigenetic effects.[76] And yet, we are applying these products directly to our skin every day! So don't think it's just females who need to be concerned with this. The most popular men's deodorants on the market also contain these harmful ingredients.

Your skin is your body's largest organ. Just look down and observe its large surface area. You don't need a PHD in human anatomy to understand the ramifications of how vulnerable your skin is to external toxins. It's a living and breathing organ; abundant in micro-organisms and bacteria. Why would you want to intentionally upset this delicate ecosystem and directly inhibit its filtering process by lathering pore clogging, bacteria killing, toxic chemicals directly onto your skin?

Sadly, it's something we so easily look past because the answers are being marketed to us on every billboard, every magazine cover and on every TV commercial. It's unavoidable at best, but confusing and stressful at worst. There's a beauty serum, a make-up palette or a concealer for every skin type and every skin problem. When you can cover up, **why bother maintaining and caring for the very thing you're trying to cover up?** *This logic is so outright backwards.*

What doesn't get absorbed into your own body is washed into our waterways. Many of the ingredients in personal hygiene and cosmetic products are water-soluble and pose a risk for aquatic life. Our waste-water treatment plants utilize special bacteria to break down biological waste (like your poop and pee). A process called 'anaerobic digestion'. However, they are not designed to treat chemical type wastes like pharmaceutical medicines (antibiotics kill these useful bacteria in the system), pesticides, solvents, cleaning products like bleach, paint and the array of non-biodegradable beauty products millions of people use each and every day. Hazardous waste products inhibit the treatment process, clog drains and corrode treatment facilities. So don't flush your unused or expired pharmaceutical drugs down the toilet. Take them back to your chemist. Regarding other toxic waste items and chemicals, take them to your local council's hazardous waste collection center (check their websites for drop off points or open-collection days) so they can dispose of them appropriately. None of these items belong in storm water drains or waterways.

Those plastic microbeads in your exfoliating scrubs cause problems for aquatic life as they slip through most water filtration systems. The fish mistake them as food. When these microbeads are ingested, they soak up toxins like a sponge. Scientists suggest that those chemicals can be passed on to humans and wildlife who eat the fish.[77] Consider replacing your commercial exfoliating cleansers and soaps with less abrasive and natural alternatives. Ground coffee, sugar and crystallized honey are all fantastic natural exfoliants that are non-toxic.

More evidence is coming out to suggest the use of birth control and hormone therapies are meddling with the reproductive cycles of fish. These hormones that mimic estrogen leach into our waterways. *"Increased feminization of fish populations (e.g., inter-sex, hermaphroditic fish - males with eggs; high proportion of females to males) has been observed in several fish populations exposed to waste water containing estrogens."*[78]

Many cosmetic companies still utilize animal testing which is both unnecessary, cruel and no longer legally mandated in many countries. While a company may not utilize this practice directly, they may be buying chemical ingredients from manufacturers who do. Thankfully, there are welfare groups out there who have done the research to make it easier for you to shop 'cruelty-free'. In the resources section I've linked to a free phone app you can download for this information. It's scary to think the very products we've been promised that ward off wrinkles, encourage healthier hair, and halt the aging process, contribute to greater problems. Stand firmer in your stance as to what deserves a place in your vanity cabinet. Never before in history is there a greater cry out for us to embrace our natural beauty and nourish our bodies from the inside-out.

To start detoxing your vanity cabinet, clear out all of your existing commercial products that are known carcinogens, environmental hazards and allergens. Don't tip them down the drain though! See if your local council will accept them at hazardous waste collection centers. Then it's time to move forward in life and work towards not contributing to the problem further.

The David Suzuki Foundation, based in Canada, has an excellent resource known as the Dirty Dozen of Cosmetic Chemicals. Their website is listed in the resources section if you're still wary of what specific chemicals to look out for. Before we get into what natural alternatives you can start replacing these products with, we need to address the elephant in the room; what it means to nourish your body from the inside and embracing the beauty within.

1. Health starts from the inside out

No matter what you lather onto your skin, there's no covering up the internal state of your body. Health really starts from the inside out. There's no denying that first and foremost, priority number one should be ensuring you are feeding your body with the necessary nutrients in order for it to do its job. Your body is there to support your health and you need to support it in return! Ditching the processed junk that one can hardly classify as "food," is a great place to start but remember, you need to replace those calories with nutrient dense whole foods. Focus on the nutrient density of your food, as opposed to calorie counting. A diet deficient in calories will do more harm than good when it comes to fostering a healthy body and glowing skin. A holistic nutritionist can help you uncover certain foods that cause you more grief than others. This could be a sign of a food intolerance. Opt for spray-free and organic wherever possible.

2. Amp up the probiotics for gut health

You can go out and buy a high quality probiotic in the form of a pill but I'm a huge advocate for adopting lifestyle habits that are sustainable and cost effective. The most effective way to get probiotics into your diet is through fermented and cultured foods. These traditionally prepared foods; such as sauerkraut, kimchi, kefir, kvass, and kombucha, brim with beneficial bacteria and live enzymes that assist a healthy gut and well functioning digestive system. A growing body of scientific evidence suggests there's a stronger relationship between our gut and skin health than previously recognized.[79] I strongly believe it is the single most important thing you can do for your skin. Don't expect that you'll be able to pop some probiotics and be healed overnight. You must start by introducing small amounts at a time (1 tablespoon a day) and gradually increasing your intake from there. Too much, too soon can throw off the balance and be too much for your system to handle. This, alongside a healthy diet and reducing stress in your lifestyle, will do wonders for your skin..

3. Healthy fats for healthy skin

Healthy fats are a must! I am eating more coconut oil, avocado, extra virgin olive oil, fish and animal fats than ever before in my life and you know what, my skin is no longer dry! *Go figure*. It's plump and full of color. I don't look look like a zombie with the life sucked from me. I can feel the difference and people can see the difference! These healthy fats also help you to absorb the skin-loving vitamins A, E and

K. Oh, and don't be scared to lather the fats directly onto your skin either! They act as fantastic moisturizers.

4. Get a healthy dose of sleep & learn to relax

The importance of adequate sleep can't be stressed enough. When your body is taxed and stressed, your skin is the first to show it. Raccoon eyes only look cute on raccoons, *not on people.* Shoot for 7 to 8 hours of uninterrupted sleep. I find sleeping with earplugs helps if I'm really struggling with outside noise. Blackout your room and remove the presence of all electronic devices. These things all affect the quality of our sleep. Incorporate stress-reducing activities into your daily schedule. Breathing techniques, meditation, prayer, yoga and physical activities all reduce stress.

5. Embrace your unique beauty

When it comes to long-term health and wellness, the only thing that will keep you grounded is a firm belief in the beauty of your soul. Beauty really is in the eye of the beholder and an ugly personality is enough to shroud any external image. Embrace your natural beauty, who you are as a person and the imperfections that make you unique. Focus on your strengths and the parts of your body you love rather than scrutinising the parts you don't. I've said it once before and I'll say it again - *humans are self-involved species* (and I say this with full respect but even I'll admit to this flaw in our character). What you see, others most likely *do not* because they are too focused on their own imperfections. Self-love is not a trendy catchphrase from the latest issue of Cosmo. It's a daily practise of self-acceptance and celebration that traces to the origins of man. Through this, you permit yourself to live authentically and richly.

Here are my five favorite natural "products" for healthy skin.

Raw honey

Honey has anti-microbial and anti-fungal properties. It's nature's liquid gold. In its crystallized form, honey also acts as a gentle exfoliator when applied with a splash of water. So simple and yet so effective. Be sure to buy raw honey, not the pasteurized stuff on the supermarket shelves. You can be sure to lick your lips with this one!

Apple cider vinegar (diluted with water)

ACV should be a staple in every kitchen pantry but its utility extends beyond that. It's a fantastic toner that helps to maintain your skin's natural PH level which in turn, supports your skin's integrity. Coupled with antibacterial and anti-fungal properties, it can be used to help dry excess oils and remove other skin and make-up products that clog pores. ACV can be harsh and sting if applied directly to the skin so dilute one part ACV to three parts water and keep away from your eyes. For those who suffer from acne or sensitive, it should be used sparingly at a ratio of 1:10. Apply using a make-up pad or cotton ball after your wash your face. You needn't wash it off can can apply a moisturiser directly after.

Jojoba oil

I am in love with this stuff and it's become my go-to moisturizer. Jojoba oil is extracted from the plant's seed and is known to mimic the natural sebum produced by our skin. It's highly shelf-stable and unlikely to go rancid unlike less stable vegetable and seed oils. It's also high in vitamin A, B1, B2, B6 and E - all skin health promoting vitamins!

Rosehip seed oil

This oil has a pleasant nutty smell and works on the cellular level to rejuvenate skin cells. It feels like silk when you apply it and a little goes a long way. I love to use it under my eyes to reduce dark circles, lines and puffiness.

Cold water

Sometimes it's the simplest things that are the most effective! A splash of cold water on your face in the morning immediately wakes you up and revitalizes your skin cells. I steer clear of washing my face with hot water or steam as it can produce redness, inflammation and even broken capillaries.

Other beauty tips and tricks worth a look include the Oil Cleansing Method and 'no-poo shampoo' which are mentioned to in the resources section.

Revamp your beauty and personal hygiene routine with these tips to reduce your costs and environmental impact:

- When it comes to female hygiene, forgo disposable tampons and pads whenever possible. One of the greatest investments you can make is a reusable menstrual cup (brands like Diva Cup and Moon Cup) and washable cloth pads. These alone can save you hundreds of dollar over the course of your fertile life.

- Replace your disposable razors with replaceable razor heads. Forgo the shaving creams and just use water (not running water of course) or a natural oil like olive or coconut oil.

- For the love of water, learn to shower in under 3 minutes. At the very least, turn your the tap off when you shampoo, shave and brush your teeth. Save money by using cold water when possible and only use hot water if necessary.

- Purchase 100% biodegradable body lotions and washes if you don't want to make your own.

- Opt for biodegradable toilet paper made from 100% post-consumer waste.

- Dispose of hazardous waste at council collection centers.

- Do not flush baby wipes, female hygiene products, drugs, chemicals and inorganic matter down the drain.

CHAPTER 31

Rehabilitate the Gym Junkie

"The average gym junkie today is all about appearance, not ability. Flash, not function. These men may have big, artificially pumped up limbs, but all that the size is in the muscle tissue; their tendons and joints are weak. Ask the average muscleman to do a deep one-leg squat-ass-to-floor-style-and his knee ligaments would probably snap in two. What strength most bodybuilders do have, they cannot use in a coordinated way; if you asked them to walk on their hands they'd fall flat on their faces."
- Paul Wade, Author of 'Convict Conditioning'

I am probably the last standing human on this planet (or at the very least, in the privileged world of the West) who has never owned a gym membership card. *And I'm in my twenties.* According to Instagram, this is prime time to sport crop tops and butt-revealing short-shorts in an attempt to woo other muscle-bulging, weight-pumping gym junkies. *Supposedly.* I've never been good at following the expectations of society though, let alone participating in the sport of 'wooing'.

While I'll never turn down the opportunity to sneak a peek at some washboard abs, I by no means see these as being the pinnacle of health and wellness and something we should all strive towards. Please don't reduce your self-worth to that level. Beyond the six-pack, sometimes there's little more than a six-pack of empty beer cans and a rather insecure individual.

A gym junkie can be defined as someone who harbors an attitude of the *bigger* the *better*. The *leaner*, the *healthier*. The *harder*, the more *effective*. **No pain, no gain**. *You get the drift.* You may not even be a 'gym-junkie' *per se,* but you may be caught up in the glorification of exercise obsession.

How do you know if you have taken this obsession a little too far?

You tear half your T-shirts when you flex. The simple process of leaning over to pick something up brings about beads of sweat either because you fear that wretched tearing sound again, or you can't quite reach because (say this in a Schwarzenegger voice) *muscles-too-big-and-too-tight*. You're muscularly sore 90% of the week and find yourself with far more injuries now than prior to your gym junkie days but that's okay because you're "in training" (but you are never quite sure what the heck you are training for). You forgo social interaction with people outside of your junkie circle because they just don't understand. Your priority for the week (and life goals in general) revolve around upping your reps, or lifting heavier. You fear fat because it may cover up those hard earned washboard abs. And because you're constantly "in training", you have socially alienated yourself.

Exercise is more than a series of repetitive motions for physical or emotional torture and calorie burning. It's an opportunity to practice movement that strengthens your body for overall wellness and a sustainable physicality that will prevent injury in the future. The aesthetics are a by-product. *Not the end goal.* Often the mere mention of the word "exercise" sends people into a mass of sweat. By approaching it as a form of movement and play, you detach these negative connotations associated with exercise. Movement is any type of muscle contraction, such as walking around the office or even gardening. Exercise in the mainstream sense (and in particular, long bouts of cardio) can be *extremely* stressful on the body. Those hours of running on concrete are terrible for your joints! It's not a long term solution for sustainable health.

Truth bomb alert. My natural inclination to stay clear of gyms originally didn't stem from a place of environmental concern. I know right. **SHOCK HORROR.** I held this view prior to my 'greenie' days. I've never felt comfortable in gyms and was always too stingy to pay someone else for the privilege to exercise in the containment of their four walls. It just feels so... *unnatural.* We spend enough hours of the days cooped up inside, I really didn't need another reason. On a couple occasions, I was dragged through the doors wielding the power of a free courtesy pass at the insistence of a friend. Like a kid with her mouth open on a Dentist chair, I didn't want to be there. I'm sure many people have felt this uneasiness.

Do I hate on people who choose to exercise at the gym? No, *of course not.* **I don't hate on anybody.** *Only the little magical Leprechauns who are to blame for cursing people with ignorance.*

Most gyms are large scale, inefficient, energy hungry factories with human guinea pigs running the treadmills. Mentally, I find this the most abusive form of exercise out there. The average treadmill uses 1500 watts of energy.[80] If utilized for 30 minutes, you're looking at around 0.75 KWH. If the cost of electricity is 30 cents (based on a rough average of current prices in Australia), and you use the machine 30 minutes everyday, you're spending nearly $7 a month to keep it running. For a single gym, it certainly adds up. For the individual who owns their own treadmill, by about the third year mark, you'll have spent more on electricity than you did on buying the original machine and probably little weight loss to show for it.

The manufacturing of these exercise machines are also a resource intensive process. Think about the steel, plastic and rubber. Then these machines need to be maintained and as they age, they'll need to be replaced. Their life-cycle is usually short lived if not replaced to keep up with the moving trends and technology advancements.

In some instances, it doesn't matter whether there's one person or one

155

hundred people working out. The gym maintains the air conditioning cycle, powering the plasma TV screens and the countless exercise machines in standby mode that draw power from the grid even if not in operation. Couple that with the number of attendees who drive there - it's all rather backwards. *Paying someone else so you can burn calories and burn electricity in the process?*

You are paying for this exclusive right to use energy to *burn energy.* Or maybe you aren't because you are one of the 67% of us who pay for these services and never use them.[81] It's a $75 billion industry. This is BIG business. The average gym membership runs at about $50-$60 a month. Unless you have a very specific goal in mind (like a competitive athlete), or require the direction and motivation from a personal trainer, **you're paying to consume energy.** It just doesn't add up.

An unused gym membership is enough money to buy healthier, organic food each week so you don't have to work so hard to punish yourself to burn off those calories. Or you could use that money to fund more emotionally rewarding exercise experiences like outdoor hiking, walking your dog, yoga in the park, gardening to grow your own food or playing Frisbee with the kids. Oh wait, *those don't cost anything.*

I think it's high time we question what other form of productive movement we can be doing that is both more sustainable and better for our physical and mental wellness. There's a slight tingling in my belly that tells me we're not akin to rats on an exercise wheel and our bodies don't respond so positively to this experience. While there's nothing wrong with targeted muscle training, many alternatives exist that are environmentally friendly, accessible and more emotionally rewarding. If you're one of the many who find the gym a soul-sucking experience, you don't need to force yourself to join the rate race just because others have. These other options are worth exploring if you have an open mind to saving your sanity, carbon consumption and MONEY!

1. Outdoor adventure

Think mountain hiking, kayaking, rock climbing and nature trails. What better way to exercise than under the beautiful rays of the sun where you get the chance to soak up some extra Vitamin D that will do your body a host of health wonders. Connecting with nature will also nurture your spiritual, emotional and mental well-being. You even get the opportunity to socialize in the process and explore a new corner of your surrounding natural landscapes you may have never known existed. Other than any equipment you will require which you can always buy second hand or borrow, these activities are all FREE!

2. Yoga

I'm biased here because yoga has somewhat transformed my life. The gentle and yet stimulating exercise of yoga flows have amazing health benefits for the mind, soul and serious body strength and balance. You can partake in yoga anywhere and everywhere. You can attend a few classes to get yourself oriented with optimal postures and sequences. While some forms of yoga classes are adjoined to gyms, there are independent studios out there that practice with a roof over their heads or even in city parks. You can easily practice at home or outdoors with friends.

3. Crossfit

While I'm not a Crossfit junkie myself and at times it may even resemble the beginnings of a cult (although I'm sure it's not), I do believe in the power of high intensity, minimalist workouts as they relate more to the natural human experience. I appreciate the no frills approach to these warehouse-like structures. The equipment is fairly straight forward and you won't see any treadmills. Also, I love the fact that many attendees and workers embrace a wholesome and healthy lifestyle as part of the bigger picture. I've even seen some of these facilities up the ante on eco-friendly, using recycled and second hand equipment like tyres, wooden boxes, weights and ropes. Use this as inspiration to make your own crossfit gym at home or with friends.

4. Farming/Gardening/Labor

Oh yes. THIS has got to be my favorite recommendation of all. Place a shovel in the hands of every gym junkie and get them outside digging some garden beds and we could be onto something. Large rocks are nature's natural weights.

5. Play

Play can be exercise and you get to have fun in the process. It really is a winning combination. Get outside and chase the kids. Go walk the dog. Round up the neighbors and have a friendly game of basketball down at the park. Fresh air, sunshine, socializing and movement. You can't go wrong.

6. Green gyms

Some gyms are adopting alternative, conscience and innovative ways to adopt sustainable practices in our modern world. I get that some people live in Arctic-like conditions for half the year and the comfort of exercising indoors saves the risk of losing a few toes outside in the blizzard. The particular gyms in mention are ones like 'The Green Microgym' in Portland, Oregon, that utilizes exercise equipment to harness human power to generate energy. Other 'green' gyms are popping up in the form of outdoor gyms, usually funded by the local council and found in public parks. Bonus points for exercising outside and absorbing Vitamin D (clearly not mid-blizzard though).

7. Social sport

Band together friends and form a sporting team. Social sports not only open the way for fun and laughs - you build other indispensable skills like teamwork, leadership and communication. Did I mention the social interaction part of this? Most cities, if not all, have some kind of organized social sporting league. Think touch football, basketball, softball, baseball, there's something for everyone. My Grandma is reaching towards 100 years and she still stands as number one at her local croquet club. Mind you, she's outlived her more serious competitors but even the young ones stand no chance against her skill level. *So what's your excuse again?*

If you cringe at the thought of waking up at 5am every morning to drag your feet around a few blocks in toe-freezing temperatures because your internal drill sergeant demands that this is the only way to get fit and healthy, it's time to rethink your approach to exercise. Don't fall victim to this mentality if you don't extract any joy from this form of exercise. There are plenty of ways to incorporate movement into your everyday life for the benefit of your health without driving yourself to emotional and physical burnout in the process.

If you struggle to find time to exercise, incorporate movement into your daily habits. Find opportunities for unstructured movement in everything you do. Walk the stairs instead of the elevator. Take the long route to work if you are walking or bicycling. Walk to the markets. Do yoga while waiting for your dinner to cook. Get out and garden. Lift heavy things often. Use your weekends to play more. Where you find a form of movement that you can enjoy, you'll be more inclined to stick with the habit. This is more sustainable for your health and wellness than dragging your body through breakdowns, injuries and torture. *Do what makes you happy.* There's no value in slogging away for hours exercising if your body and mind is tortured. There are countless opportunities for alternative forms of movement without the heavy carbon footprint.

CHAPTER 32

Spirit Funk: You Don't Need To Be A Yogi Jedi Master

"Being spiritual has nothing to do with what you believe and everything to do with your state of consciousness."
- Eckhart Tolle, Author of 'A New Earth' and 'The Power of Now'

Spiritual health comes in as many shades as there are the color gray. You don't need to be a psychic, religious devotee, spirit junkie or a tree-hugging hippie to participate in the practice of introspection and self-reflection. While I have my own set of beliefs, I have made the deliberate decision to exclude them from this book as I respect that you may have yours. As I've mentioned in earlier chapters, the instigation of change must come from within you. This we can all agree on. Within the busyness of modern living, we rarely allow ourselves time to breathe, to check in with ourselves to see how we are feeling, and to take a moment to say a short prayer of thanks and gratitude to what we have been blessed with in our lives. Doing these simple things help promote an internal health of the mind that benefits long term wellness.

In nurturing this innate desire for spiritual connection with each other and the world around us, we build inner strength. Have you been in the presence of someone who emits a warm, calm and peaceful presence? It's a natural sensation we can all experience in our own lives regardless if you are an introvert or extrovert. Taking small snippets of time from your daily routine for these moments of self reflection and solitude provide you with the opportunity to obtain feedback from your body, mind and surroundings. Feedback you can use to process your emotions, to think through the day and to allow all of that to just sit and be. This needn't involve being sworn in as a

160

monk and to stop, drop and pray five times a day. It's a personal relationship between you and the world around you.

Meditating and nurturing this softer and more vulnerable side to your being involves expressing gratitude for what you have. It could be something you do on a morning walk, while you garden, sitting in silence in bed when you first wake, or as part of your yoga practice. I prefer to take a moment to meditate while not doing anything else when I first wake up in preparation for the day and before I go to bed as a way to empty my thoughts in closing. To you, this "meditation" may look different. For me, it's rather simple. I sit, and I am still. Sometimes I lay down. I do not seek spiritual enlightenment, but a moment to be still and present. To smell, to listen, to breathe deeply and take in my surroundings. It's an energy-producing practice. Throughout the day I also spend moments in and out of prayer.

This practice has taught me to not get hung up on perfection but rather, seek consistency throughout all aspects of life. These daily practices help to reduce stress and are powerful catalysts for new ideas, happiness and change in your life.

PART 6

PRINCIPLE 4
TO SHARE WITH THE COMMUNITY

CHAPTER 33

The Power of Partnership and Community

"A sustainable world means working together to create prosperity for all."
- Jacqueline Novogratz, Entrepreneur and Author

Community and acceptance weaves humans together. Even Adam needed a partner in the Garden of Eden in the form of his partner in crime, Eve. Not much has changed some thousands of years later. It's part of our human make up that we crave affection, connection and that all quintessential feeling of belonging.

I've yet to meet someone who claims they prefer the company of their 'things' over the company of loved ones. Whether that be children, family, friends or even pets. Even as an introvert, you still need connection with the world around you. We seek these meaningful connections in order to make sense of this world. To feel like what we are doing *means* something and having others acknowledge our efforts and presence in the process.

While meeting new people brings about bouts of sweat and hypertension for some, once you've found your tribe, it's hard to imagine a life without them. These people are your soundboard for life's problem, a warm pillow of comfort, a bucket of fun and a support network in every sense of the word. Focus your attention on building up these communities that will strengthen not only you, but the world around you. Through the power of numbers, there's greater potential for a more impacting presence.

There is a flip side though. An inherent problem with the social constructs of our communities, is that every part of our lives has become segmented and segregated. This is a common trait across modern societies that is less prevalent in many traditional cultures. Where the family home was once a meeting point for both business, family and socializing, it's now become a deserted place where the occasional family meal takes place and we retreat for slumber if we're fortunate enough to get away from the office. The same can be said for community spaces at large. Sadly, people suffer to the hands of this compartmentalization because where one world ends, another begins but rarely do they overlap.

I do not imply we should bring our work (and all the stress and problems that come with that) home with us. Firstly, we are privileged to have the space and the money to afford such compartmentalization in our lives. In many societies around the world, they lack even the 'privacy' of their own space; a home to call their own. They share this space with countless other members of their community and even with people outside of their biological family. It's not uncommon in many Asian, Latin and African communities for households to be multi-generational. In these cultures, children are often your insurance in retirement!

Many of us have our own homes and properties that are ours and respectfully so. Our concept of space and privacy though is so ingrained in our modern lives, we often consider it as a *right* with an "at all cost" attitude. The neighbor's tree is overhanging your fence? Time to call in police enforcement. The little rascals from next door kicked their football into our backyard again? This time *they're not getting it back*. Rather ridiculous, no? And yet these scenarios (and worse) are daily occurrences and broadcasted on television's current affair programs as though they're the bane of our existence.

This separation from our neighbors, where we imprison ourselves within the confines of our four walls and sky high fences, does little for building community morale and trust. It encourages fear and erects not only physical barricades but mental ones as well. Many communities are constructed on this premise assuming that this is what people want. We fail to acknowledge that this is reinforcing these mental attitudes. They do little to challenge these ideas and provide few opportunities for alternatives because that would upset the status-quo. A lack of open-spaced and accessible communal areas, where boundaries (both physical and social) are challenged, opens our minds and hearts to greater opportunities for community building tearing down social segregation.

An element of personal security does come into play here but why not talk to your neighbors first before passing judgment? Discover who they are, whether you have mutual interests and if there are ways you can help each other. Integrate parts your of life with an aspect of community where it makes sense.

Communal and shared housing lessens both the financial and environmental burden of human housing. As the cost of living steepens, many people (and not just students) find it economically viable to co-tenant a house. By default, this decreases your personal burden on the planet as it minimizes the individual facilities needed to support a modern lifestyle. Even housing communities that have shared spaces, like gardens and entertainment facilities can save you money and lower your carbon footprint. They not only open the gate for a more community-oriented mindset, but the workload of maintaining these areas can be dispersed among community members to save everyone time and energy. You can find companionship in these projects.

Urban environments are the way of the future so you better get use to this concept of literally living on top of each other and having your personal space encroached upon. With increasing population densities shifting to these man-made landscapes, we have no choice but to integrate the melting pot of culture and holistic thinking into the formation of our communities. What people need to understand, **is that change is inevitable.** We need to be flexible and prepared for this change and the only way to ensure our survival, is to have the support of your community. Whilst urban living comes with plenty of downsides, we have so much to gain from living in close proximity to others. Greater opportunities for cultural diversity. Amazing cross-cultural conversations and integration. Faster advances in technology and the rapid diffusion of knowledge and information. Drawing from these opportunities, you have the potential to mingle and collaborate with incredible minds; an advantage we should not take for granted.

No one wants to feel like an alien in their own community. The challenge for you is to make meaningful and intentional connections with those in your physical proximity. Strengthening communal ties will build resilience into the threads of your local fabric. Here are some ideas:

- Organize a backyard blitz team where members each get the privilege of having everyone come to their house and work on a project in the yard. The recipient can be rotated from week to week or month to month so everyone can mutually benefit from the task-force.

- Arrange a car-pooling service between colleagues to get to and from work for those traveling a similar route. America's average occupancy rate of private vehicles has fallen in the last 30 years to just 1.55.[82] Significant cost and energy savings are to be made if you rotate the responsibility between drivers.

- Organize a weekly social potluck dinner with hosting duties rotated between friends rather than getting take-out.

- Take turns to babysit each others' children once a week like a collective daycare system.

- Get involved in a local community gardens. As more cities are being acknowledged as 'food deserts', whereby they don't have access to fresh produce, the need for innovative urban farms and community gardens are becoming more evident. These projects bolster the health and wellness of participants. The growing investment of infrastructure in our urban neighborhoods and declining access to green spaces gives a wider appeal to shared interests in starting up urban community gardens.

- Participate in a community rally, raise funds to lift a new project off the ground, or volunteer for charity. These activities are powerful movers in social change.

- Jump online to websites like meetup.com, and search for groups in your area of like-minded individuals who have organized events you can sign-up for.

CHAPTER 34

You Blocked Me On Facebook and Now You're Going to Live

"Social networking platforms drove man closer to those in neighboring continents, while driving him further apart from those in his neighborhood."
- Mokokoma Mokhonoana, Social-Entrepreneur

Social Media has come into our lives as both a blessing and a curse. It has revolutionized the way we interact with friends, colleagues, business, and brands. The rapid diffusion of ideas and information creates incredible opportunities to raise widespread awareness of social problems.

There's an overlooked, darker side of social networking. Obsession with online gaming and social media have created an undercurrent of silent depression, disconnection and loneliness. People "checking-out" of reality and "checking-in" to an isolating world that sucks the life out of them like a virtual vortex. Online social platforms have also created a space for unhealthy comparisons and virtual bullying. Social pressures will always exist, both online and offline but the physical facelessness and detached nature of social media makes it far easier for people to hide behind the screen of anonymity.

Social media provides a platform for stylized and filtered living that allows people to portray themselves based on how they want the world to perceive them. You can't take it as face value. It's easy to get caught up in seeking this form of social approval but it leads you down a dark rabbit-hole of allowing others to control and determine your self-worth.

Despite the hundreds of "friends" you may have, the number of likes on a status update, who has retweeted you recently and how many followers you have on your Instagram feed, these interactions can all warp into an unhealthy obsession for social approval. This attitude devalues your self-worth and the very friendships you have with these people. Friendships cannot be quantified. Devaluing such relationships is a reflection of how skewed society's values at large have become. You need to question what and who is important to you in your life and reorient your intention accordingly. Social media can have a place in your life but be intentional with how you use it. These tools have torn down geographical boundaries and can enhance these cross-regional relationships, but the value of physical presence cannot be discarded. An active social life online should not replace your social life offline.

There's an underlying attitude that plagues the consciousness of many where it is better to be *with* someone than to be "lonely." You can still experience loneliness even in the presence of thousands. Being alone does not mean you are lonely. But being with someone, **does not mean you aren't.**

I remember a saying that suggests you are a reflection of the closest people you surround yourself with. If this is the case, **who makes up this handful of people in your life?** Do they emulate the lifestyle you wish to lead and positively influence and inspire you to be the best version of yourself?

If these people drag you down, negatively impact your experience on this planet, and are hindering you from achieving your full potential, it's time to remove yourself from their influence. Rather than exerting your effort into trying to change someone who is reluctant to change, your focus should reorient to bettering yourself so you can lead by example and encouraging those who are open to change. This does not mean you can't love and support others in their own journeys but change comes from within a person and on their own terms. Coercion does not work. You can't force someone to adopt a new way of living based on your own experiences. All you can do is live by example and always seek the truth and better outcomes for yourself. You were not put here on earth to live another person's life. You can only live one life and *that life is yours.*

Friendships take on a whole new meaning upon leaving high school or college and entering the 'real world'. No longer do these 'friendships' exist out of obligation, family ties or fleetingly situational because you share the same History class and you needed someone to sit next to. With time in scarcity due to growing career and family obligations, you are forced to practice this new found freedom of friendship maintenance. You get to choose which relationships you invest your time and energy in.

You have the opportunity to explore new friendships and discover the kind of people whose company you enjoy and your mutual understandings of each other resonate on a deeper level. Deliberate decisions can be made to spend time with these people. You find time for them in your life and vice versa. Friendships are not an obligation. The quality of maintaining a select few friendships is worth more than several hundred half-hearted acquaintances. The strengths of these relationships will be tested time and time again so it is vitally important to build up the quality of your community.

Value your own time and invest it wisely. Friendships and communities that don't serve you or the world around you should be weeded out. You will find over time this organically happens without any effort on your part. It's your own garden of life that needs tending. Intentional weeding refines your garden of networks and to produce a more bountiful and abundant harvest of relational experiences with each passing year. Friendships require effort, time and pruning. A friendship without such care will flounder, wither then die. Old friends even naturally space themselves from you if circumstances change or you've both outgrown each other in some way. Consider yourself a seed being carried by the wind to different pastures.

Ask yourself these questions. Are you spreading yourself too thin? Do you constantly find yourself over-committing and having little time for yourself and those who are part of your inner circle, that is, your family or closest friends? Are these relationships suffering because you're hiding behind your work or outside obligations? Are you the kind of person you would want to befriend because this will reflect the kind of people you attract into your life?

Set aside time to "spring clean" your mobile phone contact list and your social media networks. Connections whom you haven't spoken with for the past year are worth reconsidering whether you have the mental space and energy to maintain. These connections merely become numbers on a page and do more for clogging your mental feed than contributing to a better life. It's not that these people are unworthy but that they no longer serve a purpose in your journey and that's perfectly okay. Again, this could be vice versa so it shouldn't even be taken personally.

Your ideals are heavily influenced by those whom you're surrounded by. These relationships, and how we choose to interact with the world, impacts how we approach our carbon footprint. You can only do so much on your own. Partnerships, collaboration and support are the keys to taking this awareness and turning it into action for long term change. So surround yourself with people who share a similar vision to you and whom you can mutually encourage on each other's journeys.

PART 7

PRINCIPLE 5
TO LIVE FREELY AND ABUNDANTLY

CHAPTER 35

Mind Games: Freedom From Within

"Plant seeds of happiness, hope, success, and love; it will all come back to you in abundance. This is the law of nature."
- Steve Maraboli, Author of 'Unapologetically You: Reflections on Life and the Human Experience'

To live freely and abundantly requires you to merge your physical, emotional and spiritual worlds. It instigates a powerful shift in thinking. Let's be clear that we are not referring to the penny-pinching kind of free where you mooch off others to get by. I'm referring to human freedoms that even extend beyond human rights.

Whether your core desire to is live free from the pressures of social status and financial stress, to be free from guilt and shame, to experience freedom from illness, to live freely in a state of self-forgiveness or to live free in your personal beliefs; Sustainable Lifestyle Design provides room for all of these things. If you even glimpse a life within the realm of one of these freedoms, *you won't be looking back.*

The second part, to live abundantly, requires refocus. It goes beyond the "half glass full" theory. It involves reframing your perception of a situation from one of scarcity to one of abundance and gratitude. Rather than looking around at the world and seeing only job losses, environmental destruction, wasted natural resources and failing economies, you shift your perspective to look for the abundance of opportunities that lie within each of these scenarios. Scarcity promotes fear whereas abundance theory promotes hope. When your attention is on the negative, you will see the negative enter your life. Abundant living invites the possibility of *more.*

Thinking like this and living in this way is a daily practice and one that takes time. Your mind does not re-wire overnight. **It's a life practice.** It feels more natural for me now to look at the world and see beauty, opportunity and gracious love. Most times, it comes effortlessly. It's just the way I've reprogrammed my internal software to operate. I look to my life as a series of blessings and miracles.

I'm no different from you or the next person. I don't consider myself more worthy. If anything, I'm less worthy and less deserving. I graciously accept each blessing as they come, knowing full well, the stream may stop flowing tomorrow. This does not phase me though for I know that with each day I have been blessed, not through entitlement *but through grace.*

I still have my days where I feel like a blob of play-doh and all I want to do is curl up in bed eating dark chocolate and binge-watch all seven seasons of Gilmore Girls. You don't ignore these moments though. You sit with them and allow yourself the space to breathe and relax. Then you pick yourself up and move on with life. Coming from someone who has spent her fair share of time face-planted in large pot-holes of depression, the world will to continue to spin even if your life is in a momentary freeze.

You can't have the good without accepting the bad. The sun still rises and shines the next day, providing life to nature but also burning your skin if you bathe in it too long. The birds will go on tweeting while they shit on your freshly washed mop of angelic hair. A puppy may provide the most endearing comfort as it rolls around playing footsies with you but then goes on to chew your new $100 pair of sneakers to shreds. There are both negative and positive flip sides to every scenario in life. It's not a matter of the particulars, it's a matter of how you react to each of those moments that determines your happiness.

This is what abundant living is all about. I by no means have it perfect, but it's not within perfection you find happiness. It's through content living, gratitude and finding joy even in the mundane tasks of everyday life where you find sustainable happiness. I know this, because it's been a mindset change that's radically altered the direction of my own life. These are sustainable attitudes that don't wear off like a temporary tattoo of short term pleasure or forgotten about like that new shirt lost in the back of your wardrobe. If you can't appreciate what you already have, why do you think you deserve to find happiness in more?

When you are so fixated on short term happiness, it's easy to get addicted to bursts of pleasure. The feeling of pleasure is not inherently bad. It's our addiction and means of attainment that taint it. As one hit passes, you're on the lookout for the next in fear of feeling the pain and sadness that is present when pleasure is not. I refer to it as the tornado of pleasure. The eye of the storm provides a false sense of security but danger is imminent the moment you lose control. This is a fundamental flaw of the consumerist mindset. It's all too easy to squander your fortune on the next shiny object because you're seeking happiness from *consuming* and fail to appreciate what you already have. When you are so focused on *avoiding* pain and sadness, it's only natural that this is what your mind sees in the world around you.

Riding the roller-coaster of life requires one to experience troughs of pain and sadness but like all things, they too will pass. They needn't undermine one's long term happiness. From these moments, we can appreciate the highs and adjust our focus to what we already have. This is what abundant living is all about and how you can nurture a deeper sense of joy for years to come.

CHAPTER 36

Social Clones: When 'Normal' is NOT Normal

"Normal is an illusion. What is normal for the spider is chaos for the fly."
- Morticia Addams, Matriarch of The Addams Family

Looking around it's hard to come to a definite conclusion as to what normal means. There is no one set standard of 'normal'. How can there be? We're a diverse species. My spidey-senses tell me though that there seems to be a faint push from media, advertising, society, the invisible hand of capitalism or *whatever you want to name it*, that there is an underlying sense of normal we should all be striving to achieve as individuals. An image that is pushed onto us, as subtly as it comes. It's reinforced during our days at school. We even find ourselves reaching for this faceless ideal when we step into the corporate world because suddenly, we are surrounded by it. **Day in, day out.** Whether or not your picture of what this normal looks like differs slightly from the next person, I think we all get a sense that there are common threads. The worst part is, we are repulsed by it while at the same time being controlled by it. We're at its mercy. It drives our decisions in life. It dictates our lifestyles. We are torn. We want it, and yet we don't. It's not until we become conscious to what is going on that we realize this is *not what we want*. Rather than bending to social norm, **live** your values.

We have been led to believe that this superficial normal is *normal*. The truth being, it diverges so far from what we truly desire, to what we really need in our lives, that when we make the choice to step away from it, we are left standing in a wide open field even more confused than ever before. We are left alone, lacking clarity in purpose and direction because no one is there to tell us exactly what that should look like. So you can see why it's easy for those to retreat back to this conventional way of thinking because this process is horrendously uncomfortable. Who wants to feel uncomfortable?

Standing alone in the field, with no idea where to turn, it's also hell scary! To those who are courageous and bold enough, earnestly seeking to find their way through the wide open fields and who choose to keep walking, they are the ones who will find their way. It will take time. It will be frightening, confusing and lonely at times. You will feel tired, defeated and not caring an inch beyond your immediate needs of the now. But along the journey, you'll bump into other wandering souls. Others too who are seeking the same things. Others who are also leaving their old ways behind. You will keep each other company in these dark times. You will support each other as you stumble along and together you will find what you set out to discover.

Learn to challenge the world's perception of what constitutes 'normal' and you will start to *feel* the freedom of living on your own terms. Here are some examples of when normal is *not* normal to get your creative, abnormal juices flowing.

1. When natural, organic produce need a special label. *Apparently it's normal for pesticides, herbicides and other chemically ridden produce & products to adorn our supermarket shelves.*

2. When natural preservatives (like real sea salt) have been demonized while a plethora of additives and artificial preservatives are now found in a large majority of manufactured foods.

3. When something can be labeled 'natural food' where there is not one natural ingredient listed on the label.

4. When we care more about sitting in front of the television, Netflix, gaming and Youtube videos, than we do about connecting with people in our immediate, physical proximity.

5. When we are so 'busy', cash and time poor that we can only afford to spend our time driving to the take-out shop, waiting in line for a measly & expensive take-out, and driving back home again, rather than preparing a hearty, healthy and economical meal at home.

6. When we relegate our health needs to pharmaceutical companies and expect them to have our best interests at heart when their primary concern is making sure they have a paycheck to give to their employees and shareholders at the end of the day.

7. When we don't even shrug at trash on the footpath and prefer to kick it to the side than to simply pick it up and place it in the trash can three feet from where we're standing.

8. When we are somehow okay with throwing that trash out the window in the first place.

9. When we have no idea where the things we buy come from, who has made it, what lives have been sacrificed in the process or what it's taken to get it to us.

10. When we feel like we have a right to degrade and plunder every corner of this planet but insist on keeping our front yard hedges neatly manicured.

11. When we have lost respect for the natural life-cycle of death and regeneration between plants and animals.

12. When we turn to science and technology to answer *all* our problems rather than relying on ancient wisdom and human instinct where problems call for a human touch.

13. When information has become so highly prized over *knowledge*, we've lost ourselves to our own superiority complex and value quantity over quality, where anyone can Google the same information in a heartbeat.

14. When we are paying people less or taking them out of jobs that add real value to the health and well-being of the nation (and their individual health & well-being) but paying more to those who take away from it.

15. When one's health is being overshadowed by the sum of one's bank account.

16. When it's socially accepted, and even laughed about, to buy something you are never going to use.

17. When people sacrifice their own happiness for a faceless ideal of 'happiness', allowing a fantasy played out on the silver screen by Hollywood actors to determine their self-worth. Yes, people who act in *fictional stories*.

18. When you don't even know who your neighbor is and yet you feel you need a gun to protect yourself from them.

19. When children grow up not knowing where milk comes from, who their farmer is, who their parents are or how to say please and thank you. But they know who Justin Bieber is dating.

20. When we feel a sense of entitlement to everything and anything, including that car park and we feel we have the right to abuse that person who just took it.

21. **When ignorance is bliss.**

Society's mental attitude of what constitutes 'normal' is the definition of abnormal if ever you needed one. We've drifted so far from what is natural and true to mankind that we lose touch with Mother Nature's standard of *there is no such thing as normal*. It her world, **it all depends.** Principles act as amazing guidelines, but the application all comes down to you and it all depends on your set of circumstances and the available resources at that moment in time. When you let go of these 'normal' standards, you open yourself to a whole new way of thinking and living.

CHAPTER 37

The School of Life: Become Smarter Than A 5th Grader

"I believe this passionately: that we don't grow into creativity, we grow out of it. Or rather, we get educated out of it. "
- Ken Robinson, Author of 'Out of Our Minds: Learning to be Creative'

Having access to education is one of our greatest gifts but it's all too common to take it for granted in modern society. As adults, we must take responsibility for our own life-long learning rather than relying on a teacher, a fellow student, a textbook or Google to give us the answers. This expectancy and feeling of entitlement to an answer is so ingrained in our mental attitudes, it's extended beyond the classroom and is affecting how we interact with each other on a daily basis. We are being educated out of creativity and the ability to develop our own critical thinking skills. **We are losing the ability to think for ourselves.**

Many of us are scared to take risks and think outside of the socially accepted norm because it's not prescribed in a textbook or laid out in a clean formula. The world around us is *not* linear or static but rather, **a dynamic and interactive world**. Therefore, we need to play to the game of the world, and not to our own. This involves getting out there and experiencing what it means to make mistakes and learn from them. Life is fraught with risks and we can't educate ourselves out of them. Nor should we want to. We can certainly make educated decisions and minimize the risk but forgoing every element that makes life interesting in favor of a predetermined path laid out in a textbook case study is a fast track to a dead end of meaningless.

The pursuit of happiness in the form of false ideals of material riches, leave many young adults entering the workforce with a warped view of the world. We're taught that success comes in the form of money and your self-worth is determined by prestige. This mentality only leaves you crushed in defeat under the weight of the same churning wheel you're suppose to be helping to turn when things don't go as expected.

We need to start placing more value on life skills. The ones that *can't* be taught. Like social empathy, creativity and practical, hands on, knee deep in the trenches-like experiences. Things that get us out and actively participating in the economic circle of life rather than the economic wheel of soul defeating and earth crushing mindlessness.

Sustainable Lifestyle Design embraces the philosophy of lifelong learning. We are students of life. Education, learning and knowledge is not confined to the four walls of a classroom. It's not all about what you can learn from textbooks, how well you can memorize your answers for the exam, or how well researched and referenced your essay is. Take pride in producing and creating work of value for others and yourself rather than just regurgitating information mindlessly.

When we are so focused on the end result, we ignore the joy in the learning process that gets us there. Why do we want to stifle the best traits of man - our creativity, passion and child-like wonder? We seem so eager to trade these in for control, unanimity and a factory machine mentality. Where is the joy in the mundane; the tame and the obedient?

The idea of change and adaptation is a scary thought for most but where else can progress and growth stem from unless we don't challenge our current belief systems. Question whether there is a better way. Home in on your natural gifts and talents and leverage them to make the world a better place rather than relying on someone else to tell you where you're suppose to fit in. Continue seeking answers and knowledge and above all, enjoy the creative learning process.

CHAPTER 38

Cabin Fever: Undomesticate Yourself

"Machine men, with machine minds and machine hearts! You are not machines, you are not cattle, you are men! You have the love of humanity in your hearts. You don't hate: only the unloved hate, the unloved and the unnatural. Soldiers, don't fight for slavery, fight for liberty! You the people have the power, the power to create machines, the power to create happiness! You the people have the power to make this life free and beautiful, to make this life a wonderful adventure! Then, in the name of democracy, let us use that power. Let us all unite! Let us fight for a new world, a decent world . . ."
- Charles Chaplin, Actor

Earlier in this book I wrote about the domestication of our food system. The part where we've forced animals into small caged enclosures barred from ever feeling the warming rays of the sun, revoking their wild tendencies and freedoms to express everything that makes them animals. Have you ever stopped to look at the cage surrounding your own life? Lost in the haze of shock and horror at the industrialization of our food system, we overlook the domestication of ourselves. **We are victims to our own manufacturing**. Products of our products.

Our modern lifestyles reflect domestication; where we confine ourselves to four walled boxes in large concrete buildings, row upon row on city streets. Moving only a few feet each day and if we're lucky, exposing ourselves to a few brief moments of sunshine. From bed, to car, to office and back again. Sitting, sitting and more sitting. Eating from our own human versions of pre-packaged and processed feedlots. Watching the same dribble of mind-numbing entertainment broadcasted from the electronic boxes in our living rooms. Slaves to the wage. Working to pay off debt, to buy more stuff, and repeat the sequence day in and day out. We've trained ourselves to accept this as normal and that anything outside of this is unnatural.

You can lead a lifestyle like this and be happy. Kudos to you my friend for achieving what many do not taste. For many, it's a hell hole of an existence. We have record numbers of unhappy, unhealthy and unsatisfied employees. People who don't get enough sleep. Who lack vital Vitamin D because they live indoors and don't get enough sunshine. People who don't eat enough fresh and life-giving food or get enough movement into their day. Who are overworked and overstressed. **We live like domesticated and caged animals.**

Hidden within the depressing picture I've so kindly painted for you, there is *much* to be grateful for. Do you dare to point out the flaws though in fear of social persecution? It's possible these man-made environments, *our cages,* subconsciously draw energy from your life rather than *adding* to it. You are welcome to continue slugging away, hoping to heaven's end that something in your life will change (like winning the lottery) so you can feel just a pinch of happiness and 'richness'. But how long do you allow for this miracle to occur? Days? Months? Years? *Your whole freaking life?*

If you are stark naked unhappy with where you live, what you are doing, *how* you are living, then *something needs to change.* **You need to change.** Maintaining the exact same lifestyle, domesticated as you are, is clearly not working for you. If you continue to live out lifestyle habits that do not serve you, work in a job that you only ever bitch and moan about, and keep yourself locked up in a reclusive cage, there is little chance for new opportunities to enter your life. This 'life maintenance' where everything you do is supporting your current circumstances, is inhibiting you from growing into the truly remarkable human you were born to be. It's allowing life to lead you rather than you leading life.

Danger lies in attempting to outrun your unhappiness. While you can certainly change everything that's external around you, if there's something deeply unstable going on *internally*, it will chase you down like a cheetah and leave you as scrap meat for the vultures. This is first and foremost; where you must attempt to unlock the caged animal within you rather than letting it go crazy. It's not a question of running away from the problem. The problem remains within the fortress of our minds.

There may be such urgent circumstances that require you to push the eject button. You may realize is that this freedom can only be attained by unchaining yourself from your enclosure and daily routines. To allow yourself the opportunity to feel a sense of uninhibited escape. Whether this means moving to another city, quitting your job, traveling, seeking a new social group, dumping the abusive girlfriend/boyfriend or moving to the countryside – whatever! If that's what it will take for you to come to a new realization, to gain a new perspective, then great. Change your circumstances and then work relentlessly to understand the internal battle. Only then can you return to what was once considered your cage but this time, with a changed heart to live out a happier and richer life.

Our urban domestication is driving us further away from our natural instincts and making it more difficult for us to spend time in nature. The further removed we are from our natural state, the harder we have to search for reconnection with it. This is where we see an obsession with building up our 'nests' and hoarding things that are suppose to bring back that lost sense of life's richness. Except our homely place of peace is not within four walls. It's outside, among the trees, walking in the sunshine and within ourselves.

Make a concerted effort to get outside more. Unplug from technology for prolonged periods of time. Take the weekend off to get out of the city and go camping. Bring nature indoors with potted plants. Eat breakfast outside under the rays of in the morning sun. Get your hands dirty in the garden. **Let the wild animal within you run free.**

CHAPTER 39

The Power of Earthing: Ground Yourself Earthling

"Today I have grown taller from walking with the trees."
- Karle Wilson Baker, Poet and Author

Humans have graced this planet in all their barefoot and moccasin glory since the start of existence. Modern living sees to us imprisoning our feet in rubber-soled trainers or towering, plastic stilettos. The premise of "Earthing" is that the negative ions we receive from contact with the earth have the potential to offset the harmful effects of positive ions; the ones that instigate free radicals in our bodies that we are exposed to on a daily basis due largely to our electronic dependent lifestyles.[83] Think television screens, computers, microwaves, mobile phones and the list goes on. These technological devices generate electromagnetic rays (EMFs) that have negative health implications. The natural energy the earth emits has the potential to counteract these and aid us in restoring sleep, easing pain and fatigue.

You can spend dollars upon dollars buying Earthing mats and special EMF ray blockers. Marketing gimmicks aside, the simple answer is to spend more time in nature. You know, *outside*. Walking barefoot, swimming in the ocean, getting your hands dirty in the garden and rolling around in the grass. The answers don't need to be the latest and greatest technological advancements neatly boxed in bubble wrap.

Spending time away from electronics does wonders for your mental and physiological well being. Camping is one of the most effective ways to re-establish your circadian rhythm. The lack of artificial lighting does wonders for your natural sleeping patterns that traditionally mimic the rising and falling of the sun. Spending your vacations on the beach (bonus points for camping) provide some of the most conducive conditions for rest. The ocean is brimming with negative ions. That's right, I'm encouraging you to spend more time at the beach! Hawaii may not be such a bad idea after all.

Whether you think it's a bunch of hogwash and that my brain cells have been fried from too many EMF rays thanks to the countless hours spent glaring at my computer screen as I've written this book, it's a sacrifice I'm willing to make for the world in hope of making it a better place. Unless you're purposely out to get sunburnt or suffer severe pollen allergies, spending less time with technology and more time in nature has no negative side effects.

CHAPTER 40

Biophilia: Cure Your Nature-Phobia

"There is pleasure in the pathless woods, there is rapture in the lonely shore, there is society where none intrudes, by the deep sea, and music in its roar; I love not Man the less, but Nature more."
- Lord Byron, English Poet

Have you ever had one of those *really* stressful days where you could punch a hole through the plastered wall, scream at the top of your lungs and smash a few plates as though you were partying at a Greek wedding, *except that you're not and you have a list of one hundred things to do and not enough hours in the day.*

Amongst the chaos of such mess, it's the perfect time to stop and take a deep breath. **Say what?!** Yes, you read correctly. **Just stop.** Whatever you are doing, in moments like this, just stop. Now go outside. If weather permitting, go for a walk. Heck, even if it's raining, go splash in a puddle or two. You'll soon find yourself breathing in the fresh air, smelling the aromas of the flowers and listening to the multitude of birds tweeting. *A wave of calm sweeps over you.*

Think about those times you've walked through a forest, swam in the ocean or reached the peak of a mountain after a long hike. Unless you have a complete and utter phobia of heights, the serene landscape will melt your heart.

When we spend time in nature, it's only natural to feel calm, peace and connection to the earth. This my friends, **is the power of Mother**

Nature.

It's in our genetic make up, part of our memory response; our human instinct if you will, to be in connection with nature. This is what's referred to as 'Biophilia'. Not a 'phobia' which would see to you be freaking out in fear of something. Rather, a 'philia', that is, a strong love and admiration for something.

The '*Biophilia Hypothesis*' was first brought to us by Edward O. Wilson in 1984 whereby he describes it as, "*the urge to affiliate with other forms of life*". This idea helps to explain why we squeal at the sight of little puppies and kittens, why a bunch of roses makes a girl's heart melt, why avid gardeners tend to their flower beds relentlessly and why you can't keep little children locked up inside the house.

Our human instincts are entwined with nature and have been from the start of time. From the simple flowering of a plant that reminds us it's Spring and which plants are worth seeding for our next crop; to the distinct smells of certain herbs that bring about memories of roast dinners; to the adorable face of that little puppy that turns a person into a pile of mushy peas to the point they would even risk their own life to save it.

So is it no wonder that this invisible thread that links us to nature is one that has the potential to heal us? We can't deny that in some way, *we seek its healing.*

There are examples of biophilia healing already occurring around us. Animal therapy and plant therapy are both activities that are commonly practiced in nursing homes. It gives the elderly an opportunity to connect with this biophilic instinct if bound to an otherwise bleak and sterile existence indoors. Friends and family send hospital patients flowers in the hope of lifting their spirits from a depressive slump. Spending time in nature is so crucial for one's mental, physical, emotional and spiritual health and wellness.

Just the thought of a sunny day brings with it the hope of exciting activities. *Whether they come to fruition is another whole matter* but that mere thought even has the potential to lift my spirit. From the rays of the sun that provide us with Vitamin D and warmth, to the soothing salt waters of the ocean and the comfort of a soft patch of grass to lie on. The peaceful bliss of hearing birds tweet of an early morning to signal the arrival of a new day or the sound of creaking crickets amidst the stillness of the night that reminds us that yes, life goes on, even while we sleep.

A Norwegian study concluded that an environment devoid in nature has a negative impact on one's health and wellness.[84] More companies should be filling their office and desks with indoor plants if they wish to boost employees' moods and productivity. More cities should be adorned with trees and green parks to encourage its citizens to care for the upkeep of its streets and to get outdoors and be active. And more schools should be incorporating opportunities for students to learn and interact outdoors in order to encourage a sense of pride in the natural world and to boost their rate of learning.

Here are more ideas to get this Biophilia action in your life:

- Adorn your home with indoor pot plants

- Walk barefoot outside to connect with the ground

- Invest in a mini indoor aquaponics set up to bring plant growing inside

- Get out and garden or participate in community gardening initiatives

- Run and play with your pets outdoors (clearly not the goldfish though)

- Sign up to volunteer at an animal shelter

- Volunteer in nature conservation projects around your area

- Go hiking in nature on the weekend

- Visit the beach more often

- Exercise outdoors – don't confine yourself to the prison walls of a gym!

- Picnic outside or enjoy outdoor barbecues

- Sit in a park and read a book or meditate

- Sit around a camp fire of an evening retelling stories with your children

Look for, and take advantage of, as many opportunities to get outside. Make an effort to do it each day. It's something that is not only FREE, but readily available to everyone. If for some reason you can't get outside, then bring the outside in by increasing the number of indoor plants around your home.

Within these moments of peace in nature are some of the most powerful opportunities to feel her freedoms that are available to all. There are no questions of how much money you have, where you sit on the corporate ladder, where you've come from in life or who you know. It's a matter of you, nature and that moment in time. No judgements. The possibilities within this experience are infinite. **This is what it means to live freely and abundantly.**

PART 8

IT STARTS NOW

CHAPTER 41

The Seeds of Life: From Little Things Big Things Grow

"Your beliefs become your thoughts,
Your thoughts become your words,
Your words become your actions,
Your actions become your habits,
Your habits become your values,
Your values become your destiny."
- Mohandas Gandhi

Our needs change as we learn, grow and mature. Our circumstances change. As do our internal desires and preferences. We need flexibility in our lifestyles for such things. A sustainable lifestyle has room for these things because it's organic by nature. It morphs with the tides of life that expand and retreat.

Don't act through anger, hate or guilt. Shaming yourself is self-defeating. Through acts of love and kindness; striving to do better for yourself because your heart desires you to; this will reap the greatest rewards. If something doesn't feel natural, ethical, sustainable or even logical, then it's okay to question it. This is how you get answers and explore a deeper understanding of the world. Your intuition is a powerful tool that you can employ to listen and respond to these doubts appropriately. Take this instinct and use it to your advantage to help navigate the world.

Remember this. **From little changes, big things grow.**

For example, if you wish to exercise more, be specific and even write it down. *I will walk for 10 minutes on Monday, Wednesday and Friday.* Then go for that 10 minute walk. Your mind will accept this because it has no reason to fear a 10 minute walk as opposed to a 1 hour walk. Chances are, once you've walked for 10 minutes, you might find yourself feeling like you might as well walk for a further 30 minutes since you're out and about anyway.

Challenge yourself with a 30 day experiment. Make some of the changes I've outlined in this book and see what you learn. You aren't committing to anything long term so you don't need to fear having to adjust your lifestyle from here unto eternity. Just experiment to see what does and doesn't work for you and you may wish to adjust your lifestyle accordingly.

Another example is gradual introduction of changes. One by one, as your light bulbs burn out and you need to replace them, opt for an energy saving bulb instead. If you have the luxury of replacing them at once, that's great. It's about doing the best you can given your circumstances at that moment in time. Dedicate one night a week to a technology-free zone. No television, no computers, no music. Dine over candlelight or sit and read by the fire. If you want to grow some of your food, begin with a simple herb container gardening system. You are then on your way to a full-fledged food forest!

Habit substitution works wonders. If you want to start subbing more healthy and sustainable foods in your diet, start by substituting some of your shopping cart with fresh produce from your local organic farmer's market. Each week, look for a new food you can start introducing into your diet to replace one you're taking out.

You may prefer to focus your energy on one project at a time. Rather than spreading your mental and physical energy too thin over several, you can pour your heart wholeheartedly into making the most of one. Only then once that's mastered to a point of being self-sustaining and functional (whether it be a new habit or an end goal has been achieved) should you start a new project otherwise the earlier project does not sustain itself.

Sustainable Lifestyle Design is about finding a system that works for you and making intentional decisions about how you want to lead your life. It's not about perfection, it's about consistency. You can't expect to never touch junk food for the rest of your life until the day you die. Or being able to muster the energy to go for a run at 5:30 in the morning every day of the week. Or that you'll be able to sit still for an hour and meditate on your first attempt. If you're like 99.99% of the population, you acknowledge life does not roll as smoothly like the words rolling off the tongue of George Clooney.

It's the journey of living out these daily habits, one moment at a time, where we extract the most meaning and enjoyment. Work your way through these moments and experiences and focus on making the next better than the previous. With practice and exerted effort, you find yourself managing your system of sustainable habits that works for you.

CHAPTER 42

The Beginning of the Rest of Your Life

"In the oddity or maybe the miracle of life, the roots of something new frequently lie in the decaying husks of something old."
- Craig D. Lounsbrough, Author of 'An Autumn's Journey'

Don't be intimidated by the thought we have to solve the world's problems overnight. This won't happen. Yes, we're allowed to dream big but we're also realists. We're also pragmatists. We get things done with action. Unsustainable living has dug itself in the human psyche so much that it will take more than pseudo-eco consumable products to change the world.

The movement towards Sustainable Lifestyle Design can only come through asserted effort and action on a personal level. **And it starts with you.** At what point do you make the decision to detach yourself from the problem, as one contributing to the problem, and attach yourself to a source for the solution?

"There is enough in the world for everyone's need; there is not enough for everyone's greed."
- Mohandas Gandhi

I'm a firm believer in instigating practical changes before you have it all worked out in your head. *Learning* is part of the journey. The mind operates on a very primitive level at times and its survival instincts force you to act in fear, seeking security and comfort. You can spend a lifetime trying to unravel the thoughts of mankind; the whys and the big seeded questions in life. Many a philosopher has and many more drive themselves insane attempting to do so. We get caught in the thinking stage that we forget to do something or at the end of the day, are so tired by all the emotional efforts and mental stimulation, we have no energy left for action.

It's more fruitful for you to start *doing* something today. This makes you believe, "*I can do this*" which your brain will later catch on as a sustainable habit it can rewire into daily patterns. The mind change will follow new habits for it can't comprehend something that it has not yet experienced. Try and convince someone that a roller coaster can be fun when they've never experienced it for themselves, let alone seen one. They just think endlessly about the fear which stops them from ever giving it a go.

Empower your hands. Give them something to do. *If only you could conjure food with your mind,* everyone would be satiated. Alas, the mind can only do so much before you need to act.

At first, it will involve forcing your behaviors onto your mind because there will be resistance. Change and stepping out of ones comfort zone invokes such. The age old saying, "fake it until you make" has a ring of truth to it. Adopt the attitude and say, "*Yes, I can do something and I WILL do something.*" Then DO something.

There's also the saying that the best time to start was yesterday. The second best time to start is now. Don't wait for the non-existent perfect time. The sooner you start, the better off you will be tomorrow.

Sustainable Lifestyle Design principles exist to help you re-evaluate your life and put new daily habits into action. It's time to take responsibility for your actions and to **inspire the change by being the change.**

AFTERWORD

Mother Nature is a gift to mankind and it's a gift we are blessed to have. Within her exists blessings as far as the eye can see, as deep as the heart can feel, and as stirring as the soul can experience. Her gifts are one with potential to heal. A gift that forgives. One that can bring a deep rooted sense of peace to life. One that human creations pale in comparison to. When we carelessly destroy, exploit and stomp over her with our burdensome carbon footprints, we damage the delicate bond between Mother Nature and Man. The ability for us to live on this planet in symbiotic relationship to nature is dependent on furthering our understanding of ourselves and how we connect, relate and interact with other species, both plant and animal, in this world. There is no separating the world and its inhabitants. Sustainability of this world hinges on sustainability of the soul.

Thank you for taking the time to educate yourself about these pressing issues we face. As part of this growing movement, it's now your responsibility to get out there and start living out the change and I want to support you on your journey. You can sign up to my mailing list to keep up to date about upcoming workshops, coaching, books and courses.

Jump Online to my blog to sign up:
www.theurbanecolife.com

(As a reader bonus when you sign up, I'll send you a free guide on Urban Composting so you can get started on growing your own food!)

If you found value in what you read in this book and think it will help others on their journey, you can pay it forward by leaving a positive review on your favorite book distributor website.

I'd also love to hear your feedback so please email me at: emily@theurbanecolife.com

APPENDIX I

Resources

Inspired by my chapter on Biomimicry? The website asknature.org is a fantastic database of real life example of how we can utilize nature's knowledge to answer some of our most profound design questions.

Dirty Dozen Cosmetic Chemicals
http://www.davidsuzuki.org/issues/health/science/toxics/dirty-dozen-cosmetic-chemicals/

Oil Cleansing Method
http://www.theoilcleansingmethod.com

No-Poo Method
http://www.nopoomethod.com/

The Green Microgym (Portland, Orgeon)
http://www.thegreenmicrogym.com/

TedX Talk by Allan Savoury
https://www.youtube.com/watch?v=vpTHi7O66pI

Non GMO Project
http://www.nongmoproject.org/

Bokashi Composting is an alternative for indoor composting that

utilizes enzymes to decompose your kitchen scraps. It's perfect for folk living in the city without access to an outdoor space like a balcony or patio. For more information:
http://www.theurbanecolife.com/compost-that-doesnt-smell-bokashi-composting-city-dwellers/

Get some inspiration to make your own Worm Farm at home using recyclable materials.
http://www.theurbanecolife.com/make-worm-farm-hint-cheap-portable-apartment-friendly/

For more information on Organic Soil building techniques, you can refer to this page:
http://www.theurbanecolife.com/secret-to-a-successful-garden/

Are you interested in learning more about Permaculture? There's several books I recommend to get you started.
http://www.theurbanecolife.com/new-permaculture-start/

Download the free cruelty-free phone app for information on cosmetics and beauty products that do not rely on animal testing.
http://www.choosecrueltyfree.org.au/the-ccf-app/

If you need some real food recipe inspiration, I have a recipe index on my website to get started!

APPENDIX II

Recommended Further Reading

Benyus, J. (1997). Biomimicry: Innovation Inspired by Nature

Diamond, J. (1998). Guns, Germs, and Steel. New York: W.W. Norton & Co.

Diamond, J. (2005). Collapse. New York: Viking.

Fukuoka, M. (1978). The One-Straw Revolution. Emmaus: Rodale Press.

Gehring, A. (2008). Back to Basics. New York, NY: Skyhorse Pub.

Hemenway, T. (2009). Gaia's Garden. White River Junction, Vt.: Chelsea Green Pub.

Keith, L. (2009). The Vegetarian Myth. Crescent City, Ca.: Flashpoint Press.

Madigan, C. (2009). The Backyard Homestead. North Adams, MA: Storey Pub.

Minger, D. (n.d.). Death by Food Pyramid.

Pollan, M. (2006). The Omnivore's Dilemma. New York: Penguin Press.

Robinson, J. (n.d.). Eating on the Wild Side.

Salatin, J. (2011). Folks, this ain't Normal. New York: Center Street.

Tolle, E. (2006). A New Earth. New York: Plume.

Wolfe, L. (n.d.). Eat the Yolks.

APPENDIX III

References

1. Toma, Y., Clifton-Brown, J., Sugiyama, S., Nakaboh, M., Hatano, R., Fernández, F., Ryan Stewart, J., Nishiwaki, A. and Yamada, T. (2013). *Soil carbon stocks and carbon sequestration rates in seminatural grassland in Aso region, Kumamoto, Southern Japan.* Global Change Biology, 19(6), pp.1676-1687.

2. Department of the Interior, (2014). *Interior Releases Study of Carbon Storage and Sequestration in Western Ecosystems as Part of National Assessment.* [online] Available at: http://www.doi.gov/news/pressreleases/interior-releases-study-of-carbon-storage-and-sequestration-in-western-ecosystems-as-part-of-national-assessment.cfm [Accessed 11 Nov. 2014].

3. Cook, J., Nuccitelli, D., Green, S., Richardson, M., Winkler, B., Painting, R., Way, R., Jacobs, P. and Skuce, A. (2013). *Quantifying the consensus on anthropogenic global warming in the scientific literature.* Environ. Res. Lett., 8(2), p.024024.

4. Goldenberg, S. (2014).*Climate change a threat to security, food and humankind - IPCC report.* [online] the Guardian. Available at: http://www.theguardian.com/environment/2014/mar/31/climate-change-threat-food-security-humankind [Accessed 16 Nov. 2014].

5. IPCC, *Climate Change 2014 - Impact, Adaptation & Vulnerability.* (2014). 1st ed. [ebook] Available at: http://ipcc-wg2.gov/AR5/images/uploads/WG2AR5_SPM_FINAL.pdf [Accessed 10 Nov. 2014].

6. UN News Service Section, (2013). *UN News - World population projected to reach 9.6 billion by 2050 – UN report.* [online] Available at: http://www.un.org/apps/news/story.asp? NewsID=45165#.U63V7vldVik [Accessed 4 Dec. 2014]

7. Elledge, J. (2014). *The most polluted cities on earth are not where you think.* [online] Available at: http://www.newstatesman.com/jonn-elledge/2014/05/most-polluted-cities-earth-are-not-where-you-think [Accessed 1 Dec. 2014].

8. Madison Park, C. (2014). *Top 20 most polluted cities in the world.* [online] CNN. Available at: http://edition.cnn.com/2014/05/08/world/asia/india-pollution-who/ [Accessed 1 Dec. 2014].

9. Blacksmith Institute, (2013).*: Blacksmith Institute : Dynpages.* [online] Available at: http://www.blacksmithinstitute.org/new-report-cites-the-world-s-worst-polluted-places.html [Accessed 4 Nov. 2014]

10. Dollemore, D. (2005). *Obesity Threatens to Cut U.S. Life Expectancy, New Analysis Suggests, March 16, 2005 Press Release - National Institutes of Health (NIH).* [online] Available at: http://www.nih.gov/news/pr/mar2005/nia-16.htm [Accessed 15 Aug. 2014].

11. De'ath, G., Fabricius, K., Sweatman, H. and Puotinen, M. (2012). *The 27-year decline of coral cover on the Great Barrier Reef and its causes.* Proceedings of the National Academy of Sciences, 109(44), pp.17995-17999.

12. Egan, J. (2012).*Great Barrier Reef has lost half its coral.* [online] Available at: http://www.australiangeographic.com.au/news/2012/10/great-barrier-

reef-has-lost-half-its-coral/ [Accessed 2 May 2014].

13. University of East Anglia, (2013). *Climate change will cause widespread global-scale loss of common plants and animals, researchers predict.* [online] Available at: http://www.sciencedaily.com/releases/2013/05/130512140946.htm [Accessed 4 May 2014].

14, Harvey, F. (2012). *Climate change is already damaging global economy, report finds.* [online] the Guardian. Available at: http://www.theguardian.com/environment/2012/sep/26/climate-change-damaging-global-economy [Accessed 7 Jul. 2014].

15. DeSilver, D. and DeSilver, D. (2014). *Chart of the Week: Climate change is already here.* [online] Pew Research Center. Available at: http://www.pewresearch.org/fact-tank/2014/05/09/chart-of-the-week-climate-change-is-already-here/ [Accessed 14 Jul. 2014].

16. Estes, A. (2014). *Beijing Will Test This Giant Smog-Devouring Pollution Vacuum.* [online] Gizmodo. Available at: http://gizmodo.com/beijing-will-test-this-giant-smog-devouring-pollution-v-1450019111 [Accessed 10 Nov. 2014].

17. Holmgren, David (2002), *Permaculture: Principles and Pathways Beyond Sustainability.* Hepburn, Victoria: Holmgren Design Services

18. European Commission, *'Environmental Economics – Environment – European Commission'.* N.p., 2015, Web. 2 Jan. 2015

19. Rõivas, Pille. *Northern Europe Moves Towards A Greener Economy - Norden.Ee.* Norden.ee. N.p., 2015. Web. 5 Feb. 2015.

20. International Energy Agency, (2012). *Publication:- Electricity in a Climate-Constrained World - Data & Analyses.* [online] Available at:
http://www.iea.org/publications/freepublications/publication/electricit y-in-a-climate-constrained-world---data--analyses.html [Accessed 4 Dec. 2014].

21. Leisk, L. *How Much Do You Save With Solar Panels?* Au.pfinance.yahoo.com. N.p., 2013. Web. 2 Jan. 2015.

22. UNESCO,. *The United Nations World Water Development Report.* N.p., 2003. Web. 2 Jan. 2015.

23. Simon, Fane, and Reardon Chris. *Wastewater Reuse.* Yourhome.gov.au. N.p., 2013. Web. 10 Nov. 2014

24. TIME.com, (2012). *Breaking News, Analysis, Politics, Blogs, News Photos, Video, Tech Reviews - TIME.com.* [online] Available at:
http://content.time.com/time/health/article/0,8599,2115423-2,00.html [Accessed 4 Oct. 2014].

25. Keene, N (2013). *Force your children to keep on eating and they may never stop.* [online] Available at:
http://www.news.com.au/lifestyle/parenting/force-your-children-to-keep-on-eating-and-they-may-never-stop/story-fnet08ui-1226628969279#ixzz2WKabmomW [Accessed 28 Aug. 2014]

26. Innes, E (2013). *Parents who tell children to finish everything on their plates are 'fuelling obesity'.* [online] Available at:
http://www.dailymail.co.uk/health/article-2313581/Parents-tell-children-finish-plates-fuelling-obesity.html#ixzz2WKaySH1j [Accessed 8 Oct. 2014].

27. Robinson, J. (2013). *Breeding the Nutrition Out of Our Food.* [online] Nytimes.com. Available at: http://www.nytimes.com/2013/05/26/opinion/sunday/breeding-the-nutrition-out-of-our-food.html? [Accessed 5 Oct. 2014].

28. Fan, M., Zhao, F., Fairweather-Tait, S., Poulton, P., Dunham, S. and McGrath, S. (2008). *Evidence of decreasing mineral density in wheat grain over the last 160 years.* Journal of Trace Elements in Medicine and Biology, 22(4), pp.315-324.

29. Grainstorm.com, (n.d.). *What's Wrong with Modern Wheat?* GRAINSTORM. [online] Available at: http://www.grainstorm.com/pages/rant [Accessed 1 Oct. 2014].

30. Verdu, E., Armstrong, D. and Murray, J. (2009). *Between Celiac Disease and Irritable Bowel Syndrome: The "No Man's Land" of Gluten Sensitivity.* The American Journal of Gastroenterology, 104(6), pp.1587-1594.

31. Knivsberg, A., Reichelt, K., HØien, T. and NØdland, M. (2002). *A Randomised, Controlled Study of Dietary Intervention in Autistic Syndromes.* Nutritional Neuroscience, 5(4), pp.251-261.

32. Davy, B., Davy, K., Ho, R., Beske, S., Davrath, L. and Melby, C. (2002). *High-fiber oat cereal compared with wheat cereal consumption favorably alters LDL-cholesterol subclass and particle numbers in middle-aged and older men.* The American Journal of Clinical Nutrition, [online] 76(2), pp.351-358. Available at: http://ajcn.nutrition.org/content/76/2/351.short [Accessed 4 Oct. 2014].

33. FAO, *"Maize, Rice, Wheat Farming Must Become More Sustainable."* Food and Agriculture Organization of the United

Nations. 19 Dec. 2014. Web. 10 Jan. 2015.

34. Cassman, K., Moser, D. (2014). *UNL Research Raises Concerns About Future Global Crop Yield Projections | IANR Latest News | University of Nebraska–Lincoln.* [online] Ianrnews.unl.edu. Available at: http://ianrnews.unl.edu/unl-research-raises-concerns-about-future-global-crop-yield-projections [Accessed 7 Oct. 2014].

35. J. Bloom, Arnold et al. *'Nitrate Assimilation Is Inhibited By Elevated CO2 In Field-Grown Wheat'.* Nature Climate change 4.6 (2014): 477-480. Web. 10 Jan. 2015

36. *'Wheat Lag'.* Nature 507.7493 (2014): 399-400. Web. 10 Jan. 2015.

37. World Health Organization, *Global And Regional Food Consumption Patterns And Trends.* Web. 10 Nov. 2014.

38. Ceres, (2014). *Water and Climate Risks Facing U.S. Corn Production: How Companies and Investors Can Cultivate Sustainability* ,Ceres. [online] Available at: http://www.ceres.org/resources/reports/water-and-climate-risks-facing-u.s.-corn-production-how-companies-and-investors-can-cultivate-sustainability/view [Accessed 14 Nov. 2014].

39. Miguel, Altieri. *Modern Agriculture: Ecological Impacts And The Possibilities For Truly Sustainable Farming.* Nature.berkeley.edu. N.p., 2000. Web. 12 Nov. 2014.

40. World Economic Forum, (2012).*What If the World's Soil Runs Out?.* [online] Available at: http://world.time.com/2012/12/14/what-if-the-worlds-soil-runs-out/ [Accessed 26 Oct. 2014].

41. Brester, G. *Corn - Agricultural Marketing Resource Center.* Agmrc.org. N.p., 2012. Web. 3 Jan. 2015.

42. United Nations World Water Assessment Programme,. *Managing Water Under Uncertainty and Risk.* N.p., 2012. Web. 2 Jan. 2015.

43. Marohasy, J. (2008).*Ten Worst Man-Made Disasters.* [online] Available at: http://jennifermarohasy.com/2008/12/ten-worst-man-made-disasters/ [Accessed 29 Oct. 2014].

44. Stecker, T. *Biofuels Might Hold Back Progress Combating Climate Change.* Scientific American, 31 Mar. 2014. Web. 7 Jan. 2015.

45. Fernandez-Cornejo, J., Wechsler, S., Livingston, M. and Mitchell, L. (2014). *Genetically Engineered Crops in the United States.* 1st ed. [ebook] Available at: http://www.ers.usda.gov/media/1282242/err162_summary.pdf [Accessed 4 Oct. 2014].

46. Markaverich, B., Crowley, J., Alejandro, M., Shoulars, K., Casajuna, N., Mani, S., Reyna, A. and Sharp, J. (2005). *Leukotoxin Diols from Ground Corncob Bedding Disrupt Estrous Cyclicity in Rats and Stimulate MCF-7 Breast Cancer Cell Proliferation.* Environ Health Perspect, 113(12), pp.1698-1704.

47. Avena, N., Rada, P. and Hoebel, B. (2008). *Evidence for sugar addiction: Behavioral and neurochemical effects of intermittent, excessive sugar intake.* Neuroscience & Biobehavioral Reviews, 32(1), pp.20-39

48. Johnson, R., Segal, M., Sautin, Y., Nakagawa, T., Feig, D., Kang,

D., Gersch, M., Benner, S. and Sánchez-Lozada, L. (2007). *Potential role of sugar (fructose) in the epidemic of hypertension, obesity and the metabolic syndrome, diabetes, kidney disease, and cardiovascular disease.* The American Journal of Clinical Nutrition, [online] 86(4), pp.899-906. Available at: http://ajcn.nutrition.org/content/86/4/899.short [Accessed 29 Jul. 2014].

49. DB, B. (2003). *Insulin and cancer.* PubMed NCBI. [online] Ncbi.nlm.nih.gov. Available at: http://www.ncbi.nlm.nih.gov/pubmed/14713323 [Accessed 18 Nov. 2014]

50. Touger-Decker, R. and Loveren, C. (2003). *Sugars and dental caries.* The American Journal of Clinical Nutrition, [online] 78(4), pp.881S-892S. Available at: http://ajcn.nutrition.org/content/78/4/881S.full [Accessed 29 Oct. 2014].

51. Howard, B. (2002). *Sugar and Cardiovascular Disease: A Statement for Healthcare Professionals From the Committee on Nutrition of the Council on Nutrition, Physical Activity, and Metabolism of the American Heart Association..* Circulation, 106(4), pp.523-527.

52. Schulze, Matthias B. *Sugar-Sweetened Beverages, Weight Gain, And Incidence Of Type 2 Diabetes In Young And Middle-Aged Women.* JAMA 292.8 (2004): 927. [Accessed 18 Nov. 2014]

53. Van Gelder, M. (2013). *Green America: April/May 2013: The Skinny on Alternative Sweeteners.* [online] Available at: http://www.greenamerica.org/pubs/greenamerican/articles/AprilMay2013/How-Monsantos-Sugar-Beets-Grew-Larger-Than-The-Law.cfm [Accessed 17 Nov. 2014].

54. Foley, Jonathan A. *Can we feed the world and save the planet?* Scientific American, November 2011

55. McKillop, Charlie. *Woolworths Beef Deal Brings Grass-fed Premiums.* ABC Rural. ABC, 31 Mar. 2014. Web. 10 Jan. 2015.

56. Co.Exist, (2013). *These Horrifying Photos Show A Destroyed American Landscape That Agriculture Giants Don't Want You To See.* [online] Available at: http://www.fastcoexist.com/3016003/these-horrifying-photos-show-a-destroyed-american-landscape-that-agriculture-giants-dont-wa [Accessed 18 Jun. 2014].

57. Russel, James B. *Rumen Microbiology and Its Role in Ruminant Nutrition.* Ithaca, NY: self published, 2002

58. Pollan, Michael. *The Omnivore's Dilemma,* New York: Penguin Press, 2006

59. Sisson. M, (2009). *The Definitive Guide to Saturated Fat.* [online] Available at: http://www.marksdailyapple.com/saturated-fat-healthy/ [Accessed 8 May 2014]

60. Eatwild.com, (2014) *Eat Wild - Health Benefits.* [online] Available at: http://www.eatwild.com/healthbenefits.htm [Accessed 14 Jul. 2014].

61. Bartholet, Jeffrey. *Inside The Meat Lab.* Sci Am 304.6 (2011): 64-69. Web. 2 Jan. 2015.

62. Fernandez-Cornejo, Jorge et al. *Genetically Engineered Crops In The United States.* SSRN Journal n. pag. Web. 17 Oct. 2014.

63. Randerson, James. *Arpad Pusztai: Biological Divide.* The Guardian. N.p., 15 Jan. 2008. Web. 7 Jan. 2015.

64. Benbrook, Charles M. *Impacts Of Genetically Engineered Crops On Pesticide Use In The U.S. -The First Sixteen Years.* Environ Sci Eur 24.1 (2012): 24. Web. 17 Oct. 2014.

65. Farm Industry News, (2013). *Managing resistant-weeds is critical for farm profit. | Ag Technology Solution Center content from Farm Industry News.* [online] Available at: http://farmindustrynews.com/ag-technology-solution-center/glyphosate-resistant-weed-problem-extends-more-species-more-farms [Accessed 3 Dec. 2014].

66. Weed Science *International Survey Of Herbicide Resistant Weeds.* N.p., 2015. Web. 17 Feb. 2015.

67. Kesavachandran, C N, Fareed, M, Kumar Pathak, M, Bahari V, Mathur, N, and Kumar Srivastava, A. *Adverse Health Effects of Pesticides in Agrarian Populations of Develo.* Springer-Verlag US. Springer-Verlag US, 8 Apr. 2009. Web. 10 Jan. 2015.

68. Samsel, A. and Seneff, S. *Glyphosate'S Suppression Of Cytochrome P450 Enzymes And Amino Acid Biosynthesis By The Gut Microbiome: Pathways To Modern Diseases.* Entropy 15.4 (2013): 1416-1463. Web. 9 Nov. 2014.

69. Samsel, A,, and Seneff, S. *Glyphosate, Pathways to Modern Diseases II: Celiac Sprue and Gluten Intolerance.* Interdisciplinary Toxicology. Slovak Toxicology Society SETOX, Dec. 2013. Web. 10 Jan. 2015.

70. Cornucopia, *Stanford's "Spin" on Organics Allegedly Tainted by*

Biotechnology Funding. Cornucopia. N.p., 12 Sept. 2012. Web. 8 Jan. 2015. <http://www.cornucopia.org/2012/09/stanfords-spin-on-organics-allegedly-tainted-by-biotechnology-funding/>

71. Kettmann, M. *Cuyama Valley Drying Up.* Independent.com. N.p., 2014. Web. 5 Nov. 2014.

72. Ramakrishnan, U. *Prevalence Of Micronutrient Malnutrition Worldwide.* Nutrition Reviews 60.suppl 5 (2002): i-S52. Web. 9 Nov. 2014.

73. Welch, R. *Food Systems,* http://Www.Css.Cornell.Edu/Foodsystems/Micros %26Agriman1ref.Html. *Css.cornell.edu.* Web. 2 Jan. 2015.

74. TBC *Beauty Fact, Figures and Trends.* (2012). 1st ed. [ebook] Available at: http://www.thebeautycompany.co/downloads/Beyer_BeautyNumbers.pdf [Accessed 2 Nov. 2014].

75. Rice, M. (2009). *Revealed... the 515 chemicals women put on their bodies every day.* [online] Available at: http://www.dailymail.co.uk/femail/beauty/article-1229275/Revealed--515-chemicals-women-bodies-day.html [Accessed 11 Nov. 2014]

76. Darbre, P. (2005). *Aluminium, antiperspirants and breast cancer.* Journal of Inorganic Biochemistry, 99(9), pp.1912-1919.

77. Corley, C., (2014). *Why Those Tiny Microbeads In Soap May Pose Problem For Great Lakes.* [online] Available at: http://www.npr.org/2014/05/21/313157701/why-those-tiny-microbeads-in-soap-may-pose-problem-for-great-lakes [Accessed 16

Nov. 2014].

78. Campusecology.wsu.edu,. *LIFE DOWN THE DRAIN - Pharmaceuticals And Personal Care Products In The Environment.* Web. 11 Nov. 2014.

79. Kresser, C. (2012). *The gut-skin connection: how altered gut function affects the skin.* [online] Chris Kresser. Available at: http://chriskresser.com/the-gut-skin-connection-how-altered-gut-function-affects-the-skin [Accessed 8 Aug. 2014].

80. Alter, L. (2008). *Treadmills Suck. (Kilowatts).* [online] TreeHugger. Available at: http://www.treehugger.com/green-food/treadmills-suck-kilowatts.html [Accessed 15 Jul. 2014].

81. Statistic Brain (2014). *Gym Membership Statistics,* [online] Available at: http://www.statisticbrain.com/gym-membership-statistics/ [Accessed 12 Oct. 2014].

82. Center for Sustainable Systems, University of Michigan. 2014. *"Personal Transportation Factsheet."* Pub. No. CSS01-07

83. Ghaly, M. and Teplitz, D. (2004). *The Biologic Effects of Grounding the Human Body During Sleep as Measured by Cortisol Levels and Subjective Reporting of Sleep, Pain, and Stress.* J Altern Complement Med, 10(5), pp.767-776.

84. Grinde, B. and Patil, G. (2009). *Biophilia: Does Visual Contact with Nature Impact on Health and Well-Being?.* IJERPH, 6(9), pp.2332-2343.